My God Is Able

My God Is Able

By Rachel Hoover

Art by Peter Balholm

Rod and Staff Publishers, Inc.
P.O. Box 3, Hwy. 172
Crockett, Kentucky 41413
Telephone: (606) 522-4348

Printed in U.S.A

ISBN 0-7399-2363-3

Catalog no. 2262

2   3   4   5   6   —   15   14   13   12   11   10   09   08   07   06

To
my grandparents

Anson and Sarah Hoover

in grateful appreciation
for the far-reaching effects
of their godly example
and influence.

Contents

"The things
which are impossible with men
are possible with God."
Luke 18:27

1

My God Is Able

Alice never did know why Tex bothered her so much. Maybe it was the way his six feet five inches towered over every inch of her five feet. Or maybe it was his huge voice. Maybe it was the way his eyes and his teeth glittered. Or maybe it was the jokes he continually made about her covered head and modest clothes.

Tex operated the small gas station just around the corner from their farm. Since his supervisor often left him there alone to tend to the few customers who came, Tex usually waited on them himself when they came there for gas. Whenever he saw Alice coming, Tex would bolt out of the little office under the willow tree, his lips parted in what he apparently thought should be a smile. "Let me help you, Mrs. Martin," he would shout. "Just let me help you a teeny-weeny bit."

"I can't handle stopping for gas anymore, when Tex is at the station," Alice told Larry one day. "I know I should love him as one of God's creation, but he frightens me so much."

Larry smiled down at his wife. "No problem," he said. "I know Tex can be a bit intimidating. From now on, you just let me take our vehicles there. Then you won't have to deal with Tex so often."

"Oh, thank you!" Alice replied, greatly relieved.

So for several months, Alice did not see Tex at all. She nearly forgot about him, until one particular morning when she needed his help.

That autumn morning started calmly. After breakfast, Alice started for their little country church house. She had consented to take care of the sewing-circle materials, and she wanted to set up the last quilt for the sewing circle before lunch.

Alice had not gone far when she spied a little blue car parked beside the road. "That looks like Sister Kathleen and her schoolchildren," Alice remarked out loud. "Why, it *is* Sister Kathleen and her schoolchildren. I wonder what's wrong?" Quickly she stopped on the shoulder behind the parked car.

"I ran out of diesel fuel," Kathleen explained a

minute later. "And we're already late for school."

"I'll take you over," Alice offered. "Can you all get into my car?"

"No problem," Kathleen assured her. "We're glad for the ride. But I wish I had a can along so we could get some fuel."

"Hmm, I think we have one at home in the shed," Alice returned. "But first, let's get the children to school before it's too late."

Sister Kathleen chatted pleasantly as they drove along, and the children seemed to enjoy the ride in someone else's car. When the two ladies decided that they indeed needed to go all the way back to Alice's place for the fuel can, they did not even mind. Only after she realized that she would need to buy the fuel from Tex did Alice begin to panic. Larry had gone to town, so there was nothing else she could do.

"You can't just start a diesel that ran out of fuel," Tex informed her in his loud voice. "Won't work. You have to bleed the thing first. You want me to come along and do it for you?"

"No—no, please don't," Alice stammered. "We'll—we'll do it ourselves if we need to." Kathleen blinked in surprise.

"Well, you have to bleed it before you start it," Tex reminded her. "Won't work otherwise." He screwed the lid onto the can and handed it to her.

"That'll be five dollars. You want to pay it now, or when you come back to pick me up?"

"Oh, I'll pay it now," Alice answered quickly. "Here."

Tex took the bill and chuckled at her. "You'll be back," he said. "I might be surprised, Mrs. Martin. I might be a teeny-weeny bit surprised. But I'm sure you'll be back. Diesel engines don't start if you don't bleed them first."

"My God is able to do things like that," Alice told him bravely. Then before he could answer, she slid into the car.

Kathleen said nothing for several minutes as they drove along. Then, in a very small voice, she asked, "Did you ever bleed a diesel before?"

"Never," Alice admitted. "And I have no idea how. But I didn't want to bring Tex along to do it for us."

Neither of them said anything more until they arrived at the stranded car and poured the fuel into its tank. Kathleen eased into the driver's seat, and Alice leaned against the door. After a pause, Kathleen reached for the key and turned it. With a reassuring roar, the engine sputtered to life and settled down to a steady purr. The two ladies looked at each other in surprise. When she found her voice, Alice said reverently through the open window, "I prayed."

"I did too," Kathleen said, just as reverently. "I never heard of bleeding diesels before, but that man back there made it sound pretty serious."

"He did," Alice agreed. "And I know he'll wonder how it went for us."

Kathleen's eyes twinkled. "Just tell him. After all, you did say that our God can do things like this. This car started much better than it sometimes does."

Alice nodded. "I'll think about it," she promised. "But for now we're both late for what we had planned to do, are we not? Good-bye, and have a wonderful day."

"Thank you." Kathleen waved as she drove off toward her home.

All day as she worked at the quilts, Alice thought about whether she should speak to Tex. One part of her agreed that yes, he should know the outcome of their problem. Another part of her shrank from confronting him again. How would he respond? Would he make fun of that too? Could she stand it if he did? In the end, Alice decided to tell her story to Larry and let him talk to Tex. Having made that decision, she relaxed.

At least, she felt better until she glanced at her fuel gauge on her way home that afternoon. With a groan, she realized that she needed to refuel this car too, or she would end up with the same problem that Kathleen had experienced that morning. She almost drove past the little gas station, yet she felt compelled to turn in.

"What are You trying to teach me, Lord?" she cried as she brought her car to a stop beside the pumps. "I feel as if I cannot possibly do this."

" 'My God is able to do things like that,' " the Spirit whispered in her ear. "And be not dismayed, for I am with thee."

"Of course," Alice agreed. "I must not let my fear of Tex keep me from witnessing for my Lord."

Just then Tex noticed her and came swiftly toward her. "Let me help you, Mrs. Martin," he started to say. "Just let me help you a—hey! What happened to the lady you were helping this morning? You never came back to let me help you bleed that car."

Alice smiled at his question. "The car started," she said simply.

Tex stared at her, speechless for the first time since Alice knew him. He opened his mouth; then he closed it and opened it again. "Started?" he squeaked. "Just started, just like that?"

Alice nodded, still smiling. "We both prayed," she said, "and God must have started it."

As if in a trance, Tex slowly went about refueling her car. "It just started," he kept muttering to himself. "Started just like that. I can't believe it. I just can't believe it. I never heard of such a thing before. God must have started it. I just can't believe it."

As she pulled away from the pumps, Alice chuckled, for Tex was still muttering to himself.

Later that evening, she related the happenings of the day to Larry. As she ended her story, a look of surprise crossed her face.

"What's next?" Larry prodded. "Or is that all of it?"

"That's all," Alice replied. "But I'm amazed to find that I'm not afraid of Tex anymore. I wonder what happened."

" 'My God is able to do things like that,' " Larry told her warmly. "And I'm so glad He does. God must have wanted Tex to learn something about Himself through all of this. We often don't realize how God intends for our trials to teach other folks about Him. God loves Tex just as much as He loves us. And when we yield ourselves, God may be able to reach Tex through us."

"I hope He can," Alice agreed. "And I can hardly wait to see how He will do it."

2

"Your Sister Is a Liar"

Sandra paused just inside the door and took a deep breath. The clean, spicy odor of glue and leather contrasted sharply with the hot, dusty street outside. As her eyes adjusted to the dim interior of the shop, she could make out rows of hand-tooled leather belts hanging from hooks along the wall at her side. On the opposite side, four saddles—all handmade and decorated with exquisite hand tooling—sat on stands just out of reach of the sunlight from the show window. Behind the saddles, wall shelves held hiking shoes and cowboy boots. Throughout the center of the store were stands of Western-style shirts and leather jackets.

"Too bad no one else fixes shoes around here," Sandra remarked softly to her sister as they stood waiting for someone to show up. "Out here in the Southwest, it seems that the only people who fix shoes also make all kinds of fancy Western gear."

"I know," Judy agreed. "But be glad someone fixes shoes. Otherwise, you would have to fix them yourself."

"Howdy, howdy there." The proprietor's booming voice halted their conversation. "What can I do for you young ladies today?" he asked, coming out of the back room. He nearly filled the doorway as he walked toward them.

Sandra cleared her throat and then ventured, "I heard you might fix shoes."

The big man came forward and leaned on the counter. His face was only about a yard away from the two girls standing uncertainly before him. "Fix shoes, that I can," he assured them loudly. "I can fix anything made of leather, for sure, if I didn't make it first." He paused and examined the girls carefully. "Finest cobbler this side the Rio Grande, that's me."

"Oh." Sandra held out the shoes in her hand. "The strap on here is broken," she said, "and I'd like to have the soles redone on both of these."

He took the shoes and examined them carefully.

"Not too much wrong with these that a little time and leather can't fix," he declared. "This here desert sand sure isn't friendly on shoe soles, is it?"

"Sure isn't," Sandra agreed. "Shoes don't last very long if you wear them regularly."

He looked up, and his keen eyes met hers boldly. "Most girls don't want their shoes to last very long," he said finally.

She turned away, embarrassed at his direct gaze. "When can you have them finished?" she asked, anxious to get out of the shop.

"Friday evening. No later," he answered. "That way you can have them for the dance."

"I don't go to dances," Sandra told him.

She took a step toward the door. "Let's go," she said to Judy in an undertone. Softly she added, "I don't like this."

Judy nodded and opened the door. As the two girls slipped outside into the street, his voice followed them. "Don't forget. I'll have these shoes ready for the dance on Friday night."

"Are you going to come in on Friday evening, after such a declaration?" Judy asked.

Sandra sighed. "I don't know what to do. That is my only pair of Sunday shoes, and it would be nice to have them for Sunday. I wish I would have asked him if he's open on Saturdays. Maybe we could come in on Saturday morning when

Mother goes to market."

"She won't go this week," Judy reminded her. "Remember, she said she wanted to help Aunt Regina butcher chickens that day."

"Oh, yes. Well, we'll have to wait and see what turns up. Anyhow, that's three days away yet."

In the end, Sandra and her brother James went into town on Friday afternoon. While he loaded the pickup with feed at the farm store, she walked down the street toward the leather shop.

The big man saw her just as she stepped inside the door. "Hey, you!" he called across the room. "I don't have your shoes ready yet. How dare you come in earlier than I said you should?"

Sandra blinked. "You said I could have them by Friday evening," she answered. "It's nearly evening already, so I thought maybe you'd have them done by now."

He stomped toward her and stood glaring down at her. "I never said such a thing," he declared. "I said you could pick them up on Saturday morning, *after* the dance. Remember?"

Sandra stretched herself to her full height, but still she felt only half as tall as the man in front of her. As she gazed calmly upward at the man, she saw him flinch just a bit. For a long moment, she stood there, saying nothing.

"I said Saturday morning," he repeated.

"Christians don't lie, do they?"

"No, they don't," Sandra agreed wholeheartedly.

"Well, you are lying right now," he accused, eyes flashing. "I said Saturday morning, didn't I?"

Sandra bit her lip. "Dear Lord," she prayed silently, "don't let me offend him in any way. And give me grace to be faithful to You."

While she stood there uncertainly, wondering what to do next, James walked in the door. "Are you ready to go?" he asked. "Are you having a problem here?"

Sandra shook her head at him, warning him. Before she could speak, the big man startled them both. "Your sister is a liar," he accused loudly, wagging his finger in Sandra's direction.

James faced him squarely. "What makes you think so?"

"I said she's a liar," the big man nearly shouted. "I told her to pick up those shoes on Saturday morning, and here she is on Friday, looking for the things. I'm a man of my word. Didn't you know that? Why would I have her shoes done at a different time than I said I would?"

"I don't know," James answered. "But if they're not done, then we'll just have to come back later for them."

"Come, Sandra."

As James and Sandra reached the door, the big

man cleared his throat. "Hey! Wait a minute!" he called.

James turned back and nearly bumped into Sandra. "What did you say?" he asked.

"I said"—and the big man paused just a moment—"I said your sister is a liar. But now I know she isn't. And you aren't either."

Sandra looked at James, and James looked at the big man. "How do you know that?" he asked in surprise.

The big man considered for a moment. "I wanted to find out," he said. "And now I know." His voice was strangely mellow as he continued. "My apologies for scaring you. Anyone who lies wouldn't have been able to look at me so straight like this young lady here. Now I know there are still some honest people in the world. Here"—he walked behind the counter and reached under the shelf—"take your shoes. They're done. No, no, there's no charge. I'm just so glad to find out the whole world hasn't gone crooked yet. I hope I'll be able to do business with you again sometime soon. Have a good day now."

James made only one comment to Sandra as they walked back up the street. "What if your conscience hadn't been clear?"

3

A Special Yardstick

The bright, cozy kitchen shone with love and cheer. Most of the nooks were still unfamiliar to Sylvia, but already she felt at home here. Only two days before, she had arrived to help in this home while Sister Mae recovered from foot surgery. Tonight, however, Sylvia did not see any of her cheerful surroundings. As she washed another dish, tears threatened to spill over her cheeks. *It's not fair!* she told herself for the hundredth time. *The last term of Bible school started today, and both of my sisters and a lot of my friends are there. It'll be an uplifting time for them! And here I sit, stuck with a family I barely know, all of fifty miles from home.*

"Here, Sylvia," five-year-old Rose said, interrupting her train of thoughts. "Here's the last plate. Now we're almost done, aren't we."

With an effort, Sylvia smiled at her eager helper. "Yes," she agreed, "that's all for tonight. You've helped me a lot today."

Rose's cheeks dimpled at the compliment. "I liked helping you," she answered shyly. "Mother is reading to the boys in the living room. May I go now?"

"Of course," Sylvia consented. "I'll finish here by myself."

Rose dropped her tea towel onto the countertop and dashed into the living room. As Sylvia emptied her dishwater, she could hear Sister Mae's soft voice rising and falling as she read from *The Little Martins Learn to Love.*

With a hurried swipe, Sylvia wiped the moisture from her cheeks. *Anyway, I'm stuck here, so I'll make the best of it,"* she decided. *Surely I can learn as much about God here as I could at Bible school.* The dishes clattered as she put them into their places. When the countertop stood bare and shining, Sylvia stepped back and smiled with satisfaction. *Now, just the sweeping,* she thought, *and then I can go to bed early for a change.* She pulled the broom from its place behind the door and, with practiced strokes, soon had the floor clean.

A minute later, Sylvia closed the kitchen door behind her and started across the living room toward the stairway at the other end. Sister Mae's blue eyes met her brown ones over the heads of the children. "How about some popcorn for a bed-time snack?" she suggested. "The popcorn kettle is in the back of the big drawer beside the stove. Could you make some, please?"

Sylvia nodded and gulped and hastily returned to the kitchen. *A popcorn* kettle! *Does that mean these people have no hot-air popper?* Sylvia's heart sank as a quick check of the cupboards revealed no familiar plastic appliance. She reluctantly pulled a black kettle from the farthest corner of the kettle drawer. *This must be the one,* she thought. *And over here is a large dishpan; perhaps I can put the popped corn in this.*

Now what? She scratched the back of her ear, trying hard to remember. *Ah, yes, surely a person needs oil of some kind.* She pulled the jug of vegetable oil from under the sink and poured some into her kettle. "Now for the popcorn," she whispered. "We usually keep ours in the top of the refrigerator. Sure enough, here it is."

Sylvia set the bag on the counter and looked at it for a long moment. It had been so long since she had seen corn popped in anything other than a hot-air popper that she barely remembered what to do next. But under no circumstances would she admit her dilemma to Sister Mae. Sister Mae would surely laugh at her for not knowing how. Why, she was such a perfect mother and such a good cook that she could probably even hear if Sylvia made a wrong move.

Thinking of Sister Mae reminded Sylvia that the kitchen door still stood open. Softly she closed it. There, now Sister Mae would not hear anything.

Then Sylvia took a deep breath, stepped over to the stove, and turned the burner to HI. She measured a cupful of kernels and poured them into her kettle. *Will that be enough?* She hoped so. In a short time, the oil bubbled and smoked, and Sylvia watched, fascinated, as the kernels rolled over and became lighter and lighter in color. The familiar smell of popping corn reminded Sylvia of the home she had been wishing for just a few minutes before.

Pop! Pop, pop, pop! Sylvia glanced around quickly. *Where is the lid?* Thinking fast, she grabbed a lid from the drawer and clapped it onto the kettle—but not before several more kernels had popped and escaped onto the stove. Soon the popcorn inside came rushing toward the top. Panic welled up inside Sylvia. *What shall I do?*

Because the popcorn was nearly overflowing the kettle, Sylvia grabbed the handles and poured some of the popcorn into the dishpan beside the stove. In the process, some tumbled across the top of the stove and onto the burner. Instantly a small flame went up, and a burnt odor met her nose. "Oh, no," Sylvia groaned as she set the kettle back onto the burner. *Now Sister Mae will know for sure that I can't do this. What can I do about that smell?* She looked around, uncertain about the possibilities.

To her right, her reflection danced in the window against the darkness outside. *I'll open that window,* Sylvia decided. *It'll help air out the kitchen, and no one will know what I did.* She stepped across the kitchen and pulled the window wide open. A rush of slightly chilly spring air came in. As Sylvia replaced a lush fern onto the windowsill, she suddenly remembered the popcorn. Quickly she dumped the rest of the popcorn into the dishpan and looked into the kettle. Sure enough, a layer of kernels as black as could be stuck to the bottom. And of course they smelled burnt!

Nothing to do but soak the kettle, Sylvia decided. *Maybe by tomorrow it will be possible to scrub it clean.* She filled the kettle with water at the sink and carried it out to the laundry room. No need to run the risk of her problem being discovered.

Sylvia returned and surveyed the mound of fluffy, white popcorn. Never before had popcorn looked so delicious. But then, never before had she worked so hard for it. Carefully she picked up the dishpan and carried it to the mother and children in the living room.

"M-m-m-m, this popcorn is good," Sister Mae remarked. "Did you put butter or something on it?"

Sylvia blushed and shook her head. To her, the popcorn tasted faintly burnt. Quite likely, Sister Mae never did such foolish things in her kitchen. What would she think if she knew what her hired girl had done?

Before Sylvia could think of an answer to the question, Brother Robert came in from outdoors, where he had gone to finish the chores after supper. "Popcorn!" he cheered, even before his coat was off. "I could smell it all the way out by the barn." He brought a bowl from the kitchen and seated himself on the end of the couch. "Pass the popcorn, please."

Sylvia helped herself to another handful of popcorn. *I must remember to close that window before I go to bed,* she reminded herself. But for the moment, she was content and relaxed. Sister Mae continued reading to her enlarged audience. Rose and her two brothers listened intently and ate popcorn. And Sylvia ate popcorn and surveyed the happy scene. *Maybe, just maybe, it was worth trading a whole term of Bible school for this.*

The next morning at the breakfast table, Brother Robert helped himself to the porridge and spooned some into the small plates beside his. "I'm sorry about your fern," he began, looking across at his wife. "Somehow the window was left open." He chuckled and reached for the sugar. "The warm breezes of last evening changed to a cold north wind overnight, and your poor plant froze," he explained. "Froze pretty hard too. I took it out to the garage when I went out to do the chores."

Sylvia's spoon stopped in midair. *So that's why the kitchen had been chilly this morning!* Brother Robert had gone to chore nearly half an hour before she had come downstairs, so the place had warmed up quite a bit in the meantime. *But I never guessed it was that cold in this room during the night. And that pretty fern! What will Sister Mae do now?*

Sister Mae looked up, and her soft eyes met her husband's twinkling ones. "I'm sorry too," she remarked. "That fern was from a plant my great-aunt always had in her kitchen."

"Here, Rose, do you want some jam on your toast?"

Sylvia laid down her spoon. She looked hard at her plate, trying to swallow the tightness in her throat. *It's all my fault,* she thought, and the realization gave her a hollow feeling inside. *If I hadn't*

been so scared of what Sister Mae would say, I
would have asked for her help, and then I might
not have burnt the popcorn. And of course I should
have remembered to close the window again. So
it's all my fault that she lost her precious fern.
Slowly she picked up her spoon again, but somehow the breakfast had lost all its flavor.

While Sylvia washed the dishes that morning,
she cleared her throat. Sister Mae looked up from
where she was sorting beans at the table.

"I'm—I—it's my fault that your fern froze,"
Sylvia blurted out finally. "And I'm terribly sorry.
Can't I replace it with something? And I burnt
your popcorn kettle last night too. I'm afraid it
will wear those marks for quite a while."

Sister Mae looked deep into Sylvia's troubled
eyes. "That's quite all right," she said. "That fern
was only a plant, after all. And kettles can be
scrubbed. When I measure the fern with my
mother's special yardstick, it is not very important, even though it did come from my great-aunt."

Sylvia was surprised. "Your mother's special
yardstick?" she asked. "Where is it? I don't remember seeing one around here."

Sister Mae smiled. "Likely not. It's like this:
my mother always used to say, 'Oh, well, in the
light of eternity, what does it matter?' "

" 'In the light of eternity,' " Sylvia repeated.

"You're right," she agreed. "In the light of eternity, one plant surely doesn't look like much."

Sister Mae smiled again. "So how can I be upset about such a little thing?"

"I really appreciate that," Sylvia replied humbly. "It makes me feel unworthy."

Later, a very thoughtful Sylvia sorted the laundry and started the washing machine. "In the light of eternity," she whispered again. She stopped as a thought occurred to her. *I didn't have to go to Bible school to learn new truths. And in the light of eternity, I'm sure I'll be more blessed for helping where I'm needed than by selfishly spending time with my friends, even if they are at Bible school.*

Then she bowed her head. "Dear Lord," she prayed softly, "thank You for Sister Mae's kind words. Help me always to remember to measure things with Your yardstick."

4

Altogether Poisonous

Joanne sat on the sofa in the family room and looked at her swollen ankle propped up in front of her. *I'm not sure why I sprained it,* she told herself for the fifteenth time. Then she added, *But since I did, this might be a good time to read that book Shirley gave me on Sunday.*

Slowly she hobbled to her bedroom to find it. Picking it up, she stared at the cover once again. Something about the smiling young couple, who beamed up at her, did not look quite right. Of course, neither of them was dressed plainly, but she could accept that. The girl's hair swirled around her head most interestingly, and the young man had his arm tightly around her shoulders.

But then, maybe they did not know any other way of doing things.

Joanne opened the book, and instantly another problem presented itself. Of course she wanted to read the book—but where? Mother would wonder why she stayed in her bedroom all afternoon. However, a cover like this might look suspicious if she sat in the family room, where her two youngest sisters were playing. Joanne thought for a minute; then she hobbled toward the family room. *I'll sit at the desk and keep the cover turned down,* she decided. *That way I can be there, but they won't see what I'm reading. After all, I'm almost eighteen, so I should be able to handle this book.*

A short time later, Father came inside to do some paperwork. "Why, Joanne!" he said, surprised to see her at his desk. "Are you—is your ankle comfortable there?"

Joanne squirmed. "Not really," she admitted, without looking up.

Father was silent for a moment. Then he asked, "What are you reading?"

Joanne closed the book and laid it face-down on the desk. "Shirley gave it to me on Sunday," she explained, running her thumb along the edge of the cover. "She said this author is a Christian and her stories are always interesting."

"That may be," Father answered. "But what

kind of book is it?"

"It seems like a good book," Joanne tried to explain. "All the people in it are Christians. Surely if they are that good, their story can't be all bad."

"Really?" said Father. "May I see it?"

Joanne handed him the book.

Father looked at the cover; then he leafed through the book, reading snatches here and there. When he looked at Joanne again, his face was sad. "These folks claim to be Christians," he stated. "But I don't want my daughter reading stories like this."

He paused a moment to get a chair. Then he went on. "Can you imagine Mother and me acting like the parents in this story?"

Joanne shook her head. "Oh, no. You love us much more than that father loved his family," she said. "You'd never act like that."

"Or can you imagine Roger and Celia talking like this young couple?" Father asked.

Joanne thought about her older sister Celia, now married to Roger Diller. They never displayed their intimate affection in public, but Joanne knew they were truly happy together. Again she shook her head. "If Roger and Celia would talk like that, I wouldn't know them anymore," she said. "They're just not that kind of people."

Father nodded his head. "And what kind of

people does it take to look and act like this?" He tapped the picture on the cover of the book.

Joanne's eyes widened. "Why, I thought . . . they say they are Christians. Aren't they?"

Father shook his head. "We don't want to judge. But anyone who does not obey the Bible is not a good example for my daughter to follow."

"But I'm not planning to act like those people," Joanne answered quickly. "I can read it for an interesting story and believe just the good parts, can't I?"

Father did not answer for several moments. Then he asked, "Have you ever seen the little green balls we sometimes put in the feed alley and behind the grain bin?"

Joanne nodded.

"Would you consider eating some of those?" Father asked next.

"Of course not," Joanne gasped. "I'd never do such a thing. Those are altogether poisonous, aren't they?"

"They're rat poison," Father agreed. "But they look almost like candy, all shiny and green like that. Surely something that looks so good can't be all bad, can it?"

Joanne shuddered. "But it is," she insisted. "I've seen quite a few poisoned rats already. I don't want to touch the stuff!"

Father pulled his chair closer to Joanne. "I'm glad you feel that way," he said. "But you weren't quite correct in saying that it's altogether poisonous. The last time I checked, I found there is only one-half of one-hundredth percent poison in those balls. The rest is perfectly good-tasting food, and I'm sure it tastes good to the rats. However, the manufacturers have so thoroughly mixed in the poison that no rat can eat the good food without getting the poison, no matter how carefully it eats. Do you understand?"

"I think so," Joanne replied. "But can't a person read around the bad things in a book?"

"Can you?" Father asked. He examined Joanne's face carefully.

Joanne thought about that. "I can try," she said.

"You could try," Father agreed. "But neither you nor anyone else can accomplish it. Our enemy, the devil, is much too cunning for us to outwit him like that. Our reading becomes food for our souls, and we need to be careful what we feed on. The poison in this kind of book will destroy your appetite for the Bible and other spiritual books. And finally, it will kill your spiritual life, just as surely as that other poison kills the rats."

Joanne nodded. She could understand that.

"When you were younger," Father went on, "Mother or I checked every book you read. Now that you are older, we expect you to choose books according to the Scriptural principles we tried to teach you. But if you start hankering after this kind of book, we will need to help you stay away from the poison." Father got up and pushed the chair back into its place. "I will be talking to Shirley's father. Maybe he doesn't know what kind of books she's reading. Also, I want you to give this book back to Shirley without reading the rest of it. Will that be too hard?"

Joanne looked at her still-swollen foot for a long moment. Then she met her father's kind eyes. "No, it won't be," she said. "And I thank you for this lesson about poison. From now on, I will stay as far away from it as I can."

5

All That Is Available

After the last strains of the parting hymn had died away, Leah stood and closed her eyes tightly. Even with her eyes closed, she could see the congregation standing reverently for the final benediction of the service. *Such dear people,* she reflected. *And yet . . .*

"God bless you," Crystal greeted Leah a moment later. "Wasn't it refreshing again, the prayer meeting we've just had?"

"It was," Leah agreed slowly. "Kind of."

Crystal examined Leah's face. "Kind of? What do you mean by that?"

Leah rubbed the back of the bench in front of her. "It's just, well, I hardly know how to say it," she said. "But, um, lately I've been wondering if . . ."

"If what?"

Leah stopped her rubbing and looked full into Crystal's kind face. In that instant, she decided to confide her problem into Crystal's waiting ears. Crystal was nearly ten years older than Leah, and she would surely know what should be done. "I've been wondering," she began, "if it's worth coming to prayer meeting anymore, for not more than I get out of it." She resumed her rubbing of the bench. "More and more, it seems to me that just a few men discuss the Scriptures, and then a few of them pray, and the rest of us have to listen. And then I go home and wonder what I've learned."

"Oh, you dear girl," Crystal murmured softly. "I had no idea you felt like that."

"But I do," Leah replied. "So what should I do about it? I really don't want to feel like this. It wouldn't work for me to skip a few weeks, would it?"

Crystal stood deep in thought. She knew that Leah lived alone and that her parents did not support her Christian life. Leah had one Christian brother, who lived in another state; but beyond that, she had no close relatives who professed Christianity. Leah had seemed like a staunch Christian for several years. And now this.

"No! It would not work for you to stay away for several weeks," Crystal declared finally. "That would only take you farther from the path you want to take. Are you busy tomorrow?"

Leah shook her head. "Tomorrow is my day off from the bakery. But what does that have to do with this?"

"You'll see," Crystal promised. "It's time for me to stock up my little grocery store again. Would you like to go along with me to the warehouse in the city?"

Leah's eyes sparkled. "Of course," she replied. "I'd love that. What time do you want to leave?"

"I usually leave around eight o'clock," Crystal said. "I can pick you up at your place shortly after that."

The next day, Leah was fascinated as she watched Crystal push her cart up and down the aisles of the large grocery warehouse. "So many things," she remarked.

Crystal smiled. "Don't you want anything?" she asked.

Leah thought for a bit. "Not really," she answered. "I don't need much."

"Are you sure you don't need anything?" Crystal asked.

"Well"—Leah considered carefully—"I could use some of that toothpaste. And maybe a box of soap. But I really don't need much when it's just me in my apartment."

"I'm finished now, so let's go to the checkout."

As the girls loaded the groceries into the van, Leah started laughing. "So many things in that store," she said again.

"Yes," Crystal agreed. "Leah, there are hundreds of thousands of dollars' worth of merchandise sitting there, just waiting for us to come along and buy it. And what do you do? Why, you come along and insist that the only thing you really need is a tube of toothpaste." She stopped and watched Leah carefully. "The only thing you brought away from this huge store is exactly what you thought you needed. And it's the same way when we go to prayer meeting. Or any other church service, for that matter."

A light began to dawn on Leah's face. "I think I understand," she said. "Keep on."

Crystal closed her eyes for an instant. "When we go to prayer meeting and feel like we don't want what's there, we won't receive any benefit from it," she continued. "Isn't it almost an insult to God to sit there before all the riches of His Word and with the power of heaven available to us through prayer and then to say that we didn't receive anything worthwhile?"

Leah continued loading the groceries in silence.

When the last box had been stowed into place, she closed the door. Then she stood for a minute, deep in thought. "Yes, it is," she finally agreed. "Thank you for explaining that to me. From now on, I'll go to the church services with a determination to receive everything that I can possibly carry home. I want all that is available."

Crystal reached over and squeezed Leah's shoulder tightly. "God will bless you for that," she said.

6

"But It Isn't Mine"

"What do we do now, Dwight?" Kevin wondered aloud. "Didn't the ticket agent just tell you that our bus is an hour behind schedule?"

"Yes," Dwight answered over the hubbub in the bus terminal. "That means we have almost two hours to wait. We ought to call Brother James and explain the situation to him before he starts worrying about us."

"Good idea," Kevin agreed. "But it seems like a bad start to a new job."

Dwight chuckled. "There's not much we can do about that. If Brother James Glenwood was kind enough to offer both of us a job on his farm, he ought to understand this new problem as well."

"I suppose so," Kevin had to agree. "Are you going to call him right now?"

"If you'll sit on our suitcases so they don't walk away," Dwight told him. "And I might need a few quarters from you. I'm not sure if I have enough."

"Certainly." Kevin seated himself on the two suitcases and reached into his pocket. Then a strange look came over his face. "I have only these four quarters left," he said, handing them over. "Guess I shouldn't have bought such a big dinner. Now all the rest of my money is in those two traveler's checks that I zipped into my belt. And I don't want to get those out unless I have to."

"You don't have to yet," Dwight promised. "I don't have much extra change either, but this should be enough for now. Here is a dollar for your quarters." Then he turned and threaded his way through the crowded terminal to the telephones on the other side.

"Now, let me see," he muttered, leafing through his wallet. "Ah, yes, here it is. Glenwood's Hog Farms." Quickly his nimble fingers dialed the number, and then he waited.

"Two dollars and fifty cents," the cool voice of the operator informed him.

"So much?" Dwight groaned as he stuffed ten quarters through the slot.

In a short time, he had introduced himself to

the kindly voice on the other end of the line. "We are stranded in Cedar City," he explained next. "The bus we should take out of here was delayed; it won't come in for another hour. So we'll be at least an hour late coming into Richmond. Will that be a problem to you?"

"No problem at all," James told him. "And you boys—"

"Fifty cents," the operator broke in just then. Dwight stuffed in his last two quarters.

"And you boys don't worry about supper," James went on. "My wife is roasting a chicken, and it'll wait until you come. You'll have to help us eat it, since none of our children are at home anymore."

"Sounds very good," Dwight returned hurriedly. "We'll see you at Richmond at six-thirty tonight rather than at five-thirty. Okay?"

"Okay," James answered. "Good-bye until then."

"Good-bye." Dwight hung up the receiver.

With a noisy clatter, the quarters that he had stuffed into the machine came rattling down. Amazed, he picked them up and counted them. *Twelve quarters,* he mused. *Three dollars. Kevin and I are both out of change. These would surely come in handy.*

Dwight stared at the shiny coins in his hand while turmoil raged in his heart. "But I can't give them up, Lord," he cried silently. "I need them too badly."

"Who owns those quarters anyway?" the Spirit reminded him gently. "And didn't you use them just now?"

Dwight sighed. "Yes, I guess I did," he admitted reluctantly. "I wouldn't think of taking back the money that I paid for my dinner and using it again. So I guess this money doesn't belong to me either." Quickly, before he could change his mind, he lifted the receiver again and pressed *O*.

"Operator; may I help you?"

"Yes," Dwight began, hardly knowing how to say it, yet knowing that he must go on. "I just made a telephone call at a pay phone in the bus terminal at Cedar City. My call cost three dollars. But when I hung up, all the coins fell out of the machine. I don't feel they are mine, since I used them on that phone call. What should I do with them?"

"Oh, the money box must be full," the operator told him. "However, push them in again and see what happens."

Obediently, Dwight pushed the quarters in, one by one. And one by one, they rattled through and came out into the little cup at the bottom. "It's no use," he told the operator. "They all came out again."

"What is the number of the phone you are calling from?" she asked then. And Dwight told her.

"I'll send someone right away to empty the box," she said. "And meanwhile I'll unhook that number, since the machine doesn't accept change anymore. Thank you for calling." With a click, the telephone was dead.

Well! Dwight exclaimed to himself. *They're very careful about their money. But she didn't tell me what to do with the money I owe them right now.* He stood beside the telephone, pondering. Then he poured the quarters back into the little cup and strode over to where Kevin sat waiting.

Kevin scanned his face as he approached. "Did you have a problem?" he asked. "What took you so long?"

"No, I didn't have any problem," Dwight told him. "But Bell Telecom did." Then he told Kevin all about the quarters that would not stay in the pay phone.

"Three dollars!" Kevin whistled. "That's expensive! You mean you left it there, in the pay phone? Why, I could buy two whole hamburgers with that!"

Dwight smiled, remembering the younger boy's healthy appetite. "But the money isn't mine," he insisted. "It belongs to Bell Telecom, since I used it to make that phone call. I would feel like a thief if I used it for something else."

Kevin fell silent, and Dwight could see the struggle on his friend's face. "Maybe the man from Bell Telecom will get it before someone else does," Kevin said finally. "I surely hope so, since you say it belongs to them."

Dwight settled himself onto a chair across from Kevin. "But even if he doesn't, I still wouldn't feel right using something that doesn't belong to me," he told Kevin. "My conscience wouldn't let me do it."

Kevin stared at something behind Dwight. Curious, Dwight turned around to see what was so strange. Sure enough, a longhaired young man and his girlfriend stood beside the pay phones. Even from across the terminal, the triumph on the man's face was unmistakable as he poked his finger into one of the telephones and brought out a heap of coins.

"Three dollars!" his friend squealed, and her voice carried clearly to the two boys watching them. "Great! Now you can buy me another beer." They disappeared through the rotating door into the sunshine outside.

Kevin made a move as if to follow them. Quickly Dwight put up his hand. "No, no. Let them go," he said.

"But the money," Kevin argued. "They're going to spend it unwisely, and it isn't theirs at all."

"It's not mine either," Dwight explained again. "So what are we worried about? God saw that money there, and He allowed that couple to find it before the rightful owner found it. Can't we believe that His wisdom is better than ours?"

Slowly Kevin sat down again. "I admire your conscience, Dwight," he admitted. "I would never have been strong enough to pass this test like you did."

"That strength isn't mine either," Dwight told him. "I couldn't have done it without God's grace, which enabled me."

Kevin nodded. "I know," he said. Then he added, "We'll be working together for the next year or so. Will you help me to grow so that I can be strong like you?"

Dwight reached over and laid his hand on Kevin's knee. "Only God and you can make you grow," he answered. "But I'll help you all I can. And I'm sure you'll have to help me sometimes too."

Kevin sighed. "I can't imagine how. But I'm going to try to be the good example to others that you've been to me."

7

By Way of the Bridge

After lunch on Sunday, Kevin helped his wife with the dishes. Then he said, "Now that spring is here, I'm going to take a hike along the river this afternoon. Do you want to come along?"

Laura smiled at him from where she was wiping the table. "I don't think I will," she replied. "I'll stay with the twins and see if I can finish that letter to my mother." Then she added, "But you go and enjoy yourself. It looks like a beautiful day for a hike."

"Thank you," Kevin replied. "I'm looking forward to seeing what the back part of this farm looks like, now that we've lived here a whole month." He grinned at his wife as he went out the door.

For over an hour, Kevin wandered along the path that followed the river. Much of the path lay in the shade of willow trees. *Some former owner must have planted these beside the river,* Kevin decided. *I doubt if this line of trees would naturally follow the river for so long without having been planted.* The sound of water tumbling over the rapids downstream blended with the birdsongs above. Then he came to a place where the path widened into a small meadow.

Hmm, I don't remember this rock outcropping here, Kevin noted. *I wonder if there are any wild blueberry bushes here.* He scrambled over the large rock, searching for the small bushes he knew so well. Finding none, he climbed down the other side, intending to follow the trail again. Then, at the edge of the rock, he found a depression that was just right for sitting and contemplating beside the river.

No sooner had he seated himself than he saw a face peeking through the underbrush across the water. Looking closely, Kevin recognized the face of the owner of the neighboring farm. "Hello there, Harvey!" Kevin called. "Come on over and enjoy the view with me."

"Can't cross right here," Harvey replied. "Let me go back up to the bridge and come over that way." He disappeared into the bushes.

A short time later, Kevin heard footsteps behind

him and turned to see Harvey grinning down at him from the top of the rock. "Hello again, neighbor," he greeted.

"Greetings," Harvey replied, showing his teeth in a curious kind of smile. "Yes, we're neighbors. That land across the river is mine." Then he seated himself beside Kevin and settled himself as if to stay.

For some time, the two men discussed their farms, the weather, and many other things. Finally Kevin turned to his visitor and asked, "How is it with you and the Lord? Are you one of His?"

Harvey fidgeted and looked uncomfortable. "Well, I can't say I'm positive about that," he replied. "Oh, I'm not a bad boy. I don't drink or smoke or steal or anything like that. I guess I'm willing to take my chances when my time's up."

Kevin cringed. "Oh, please don't take chances," he warned him. "What if you are not prepared? What then?"

Harvey shrugged. "I really do hope to reach heaven in the end. I try hard to live as I know I should. Don't you think God will give me credit for my efforts?"

Kevin sat silently for a while. Then he pointed at the river, flowing along in front of them. "Why didn't you jump into the river right here and come across when I invited you?" he asked. "Why did you go upstream to the bridge?"

Harvey looked surprised. "Oh, you can't cross the river here," he explained. "I know it looks smooth, but there is a strong undercurrent on account of the rapids down the river. You cannot safely cross in this area. You have to go to the bridge. You could drown if you tried crossing through the water here."

"Really?" Kevin replied. "Well, that's exactly like it is in our lives. If we try living without Christ, sin will drag us toward destruction. We cannot enter heaven by ourselves, because of the awful undercurrent of sin in our hearts. I'd rather trust myself to Jesus Christ, the bridge our God has provided, than to wade into this life by myself and meet sure destruction. Wouldn't you?"

Harvey shifted again. "Well, if you put it that way, it almost sounds easy," he said.

"It's simple," Kevin corrected. "Very simple, but not always easy to do. Wouldn't you like to trust Jesus too?"

Suddenly Harvey stood up and began to move away. "Maybe sometime," he replied. "Maybe sometime. But I have lots of time yet. Maybe later, but not now. Thanks for the afternoon. I enjoyed learning to know you better."

As he walked away, Kevin called after him, "I enjoy having you as a neighbor too. And don't forget to go home by way of the bridge!"

8

Lucy and the Footprints

"Hello, Weavers. Lucy speaking," Lucy answered the ringing telephone. Then she opened her eyes wide at the request coming over the wire.

"Hello, this is Larry Zook," the voice said in her ear. "Would it suit you and your husband if we'd come to see your farm next Tuesday? We will be passing through your area and would like to see it, if you don't mind."

Lucy blinked, astonished. After she managed to reply affirmatively, she heard the smile in the man's voice as he thanked her and hung up. Slowly she replaced her receiver. Still dazed, she picked up her coat and walked through the kitchen, out through the garage, and to the shed, where Joel was repairing farm machinery.

"Of all the nerve!" Lucy burst out as she entered the shed. "Imagine a complete stranger calling just like that, and saying they'd like to see your farm! Without so much as a by-your-leave! And it's not even for sale!"

Joel wiggled out from underneath the tractor. "What's not for sale?" he wondered. "Lucy! What's the matter? Your face looks like a thundercloud."

Lucy pulled her mouth into a smile, but she did not feel happy as she related the telephone conversation. "Who is that, anyhow?" she demanded. "And what makes them think they can come and snoop around our place? Besides, next Tuesday is only a week from today."

"I know," Joel answered. "But don't worry about it, please. Don't you recognize that name? My father bought this farm from Larry Zook two years before we were married. You've probably never met them, since you lived so far away."

Lucy shrugged, and Joel went on earnestly. "Larry is one of the kindest men I know. He doesn't talk much, but he will likely have more words of advice for us than anything else. It's just like him to be concerned about how we're getting along, especially since he brought this farm back to production after it had been abandoned for many years."

Lucy frowned. Joel searched her face for some indication of her thoughts. "Now don't take this too seriously," he told her carefully. "And we'll invite them to stay for dinner too, won't we?"

"Probably," Lucy answered as she turned to go back to the house. To herself she thought, *More than likely you'll do the inviting, and I'll be the good little wife who makes the dinner and cleans up afterward and nobody even thanks her.* Instantly she regretted the thought. *But Joel is so good-natured,* she argued with herself. *I just never learned to be quite like that. Why, Joel would invite the neighbor's dog to Sunday dinner if he thought the dog needed it.*

Lucy paused as she stood on the front steps. In spite of herself, she had to admit that Joel's unselfishness had been what drew her to him. Why, he had been a perfect stranger to her only three years before. Although most of their courtship had been by letter writing, she had recognized and appreciated his deep, caring nature. Now, having moved into his home community, she often saw it displayed in action.

Lucy sighed and opened the door. *After all, I am supposed to submit to him,* she told herself, stepping through the kitchen door. *But I still don't like the idea of those people coming and snooping around here.* In her mind, she pictured a tall, dark man, sober and critical as he stalked from one place to the next. *Surely, such a man will have little mercy for anything we do wrong. And his wife!* Lucy looked around her kitchen thoughtfully. *The wife of such a man will see everything that has changed since she was here, and she probably won't like what she sees either.*

"Oh!" Lucy exclaimed aloud. "I have so much work to do before we are ready for them to come! This house must be spotless and . . ." Mentally she started planning what must be done before that dreadful deadline, Tuesday morning. *The mending must be done. That curtain over the kitchen sink must be shortened—it has a nasty habit of dragging on the windowsill. By the way, all the windows need a cleaning. The wood stove must be polished good and proper for once. And the doorknob on the pantry door has to be fixed so that it won't stick.* Lucy hurriedly hung up her coat and rolled up her sleeves. *I must hurry,* she told herself. *There is so much to do.*

All day she scrubbed and polished. Not until suppertime did she stop to relax. "I wonder why I'm so worn-out tonight," she remarked to Joel as she buttered her slice of bread.

"I have an idea why," Joel returned as he ladled soup into his bowl. "You've been running around like a dizzy squirrel ever since Larry called this morning. Why are you so anxious? Are you afraid that Mrs. Zook won't like your house?"

"But it has to be clean," Lucy insisted, crushing crackers into her soup.

"Clean! What do you mean, the house has to be clean?" Joel asked. He looked around the kitchen carefully. "Looks good to me as it is. You do a good job of keeping it clean all the time."

"Oh, Joel," Lucy wailed. "That lady is likely a perfect housekeeper, and she'll notice everything! I mean, she'll see everything that's not as it should be."

Joel raised his eyebrows. "And how will she know how things are supposed to be in our house?" he wanted to know.

"She'll just know, that's how," Lucy replied. "A perfect housekeeper always knows how things are supposed to be."

Joel silently spooned soup into his mouth. For the rest of the evening, he offered very little by way of conversation. His easygoing nature was not compatible with the way Lucy worried and fretted over every new event in their lives. Now, however, he checked himself to keep from explaining to her again how to overcome that habit. *Time enough for that later,* he decided.

During the next several days, Lucy kept on scrubbing and dusting. Once when Joel came into the house for a drink, he found her dumping her cupboard drawers onto the table. Fascinated, he watched her for a moment. "Isn't it a bit early for housecleaning?" he asked.

"I'll just be done early this year," Lucy returned. "I want to have at least the main floor done before next Tuesday."

"I see," Joel said.

When he said no more, Lucy glanced at him just in time to see him swallow the tail end of a grin as he turned to go outside.

Let him laugh. He's not worried about Larry Zook seeing his barn and livestock. But I'm worried about what Larry's wife will say when she sees her kitchen. "My kitchen," she quickly corrected herself aloud. She went back to sorting the drawer contents, scattered all over the table.

Tuesday morning dawned in a fantastic display of red against the overhanging clouds. Before long, the day had turned into a miserable drizzle. "Might as well stay inside and help you today," Joel announced when he looked outside after breakfast. "My chores are all done until tonight, and anyway, we're expecting company, aren't we?" He grinned at Lucy as he picked up a tea towel.

"Oh, Joel!" Lucy gasped. "You didn't forget, did you?"

"Forget what?" His face showed such a studied

innocence that Lucy nearly had to laugh.

"That Larry Zook's are coming today," Lucy said. She almost added "to snoop around," but she knew Joel would not want her to talk like that.

Joel picked up a plate from the dish drainer. "Now, Lucy," he began in his most impressive voice, "you've never met them before, remember? How can you possibly know all the things they will think of? You'll like them. I know you will."

"Could be," Lucy mumbled to herself as she let her dishwater down the drain. "But I doubt it."

As she hung up her dishcloth, she turned to Joel. "Would you mind bringing a bucket of potatoes from the basement? I'd like to make scalloped potatoes for dinner, since we'll have such a nice, cozy fire in the wood stove this morning."

"Sure thing." Joel disappeared down the steps.

While Lucy peeled and sliced potatoes, Joel sat down to read. Before long, Lucy slid the casserole into the oven. Then she turned to wipe the countertop. "Here, let me take those peelings out to the chickens right away," Joel offered.

Lucy handed him the bucket. "Thanks a lot," she said with a smile. "Mrs. Zook likely never has potato peelings sitting around in her kitchen."

Joel stifled a chuckle. Before Lucy could say anything more, he pulled on his boots and stepped outside. As she watched him go, Lucy felt like scolding him. *Will he never stop making fun of my efforts to impress Mrs. Zook?*

When Joel returned, he found Lucy sweeping the kitchen floor. "Just in time," he told her. "I see a van coming around the bend, and that's likely our company coming already." Seeing Lucy's despairing glance around the kitchen, he quickly added, "Your house is perfectly all right. Don't worry about one more thing, or you'll make yourself sick."

"If you say so," Lucy reluctantly agreed. But her broom did not slow down, and in a minute she was gathering the dirt onto her dustpan. Hurriedly she stuck the broom into the closet and went to join Joel in welcoming their guests. She shivered in the damp breeze as she waited for the van to come to a stop in front of the house.

A jolly face, topped with honey-colored curls, peered from the van window. "That's Larry Zook," Joel told Lucy delightedly. "And he looks as friendly as ever."

Well, first of all, Lucy told herself as Larry climbed out of the vehicle, *he is short and blond instead of tall and dark. Maybe the rest of him will also be different from what I had imagined.* She watched as four school-age boys slid out of the van. A little girl followed them, and then their mother with a baby in her arms. Mrs. Zook glanced around, a happy light of recognition shining in her eyes. When she saw Lucy, she came up the walk to shake hands.

"Good morning!" she said brightly, taking Lucy's hand in a firm grip. "I'm Lavina Zook, and I'm so glad we finally got here. The children could hardly wait anymore."

Lucy winced. *This lady is the practical sort, after all.* Aloud she said, "And I'm Lucy Weaver . . . Mrs. Joel Weaver. We've been looking forward to seeing you." To herself, Lucy thought, *I surely hope she doesn't ask what I meant by that.*

"Ah, yes," Lavina answered softly. "I know how it is. We've never met before, have we? So you had no idea what to expect of us."

Lucy looked at her visitor for a long moment. This unexpected statement sounded so gentle, and yet Lucy knew it was true. Somehow she could not help but feel a bit friendlier toward Lavina. Did Lavina ever have struggles like this too? Lucy cleared her throat. In that instant, she became aware that she and Lavina were alone on the sidewalk. The little girl had seated herself on the steps. Joel and Larry chatted pleasantly as they started toward the barn and the straw shed, followed by a row of small Zooks. "We might as well go inside," Lucy stated awkwardly. "We'll get cold standing out here."

Lavina followed as Lucy led the way into the house. Once in the kitchen, she laid the baby on the table and took a deep breath. "Oh, it smells so good in here!" she exclaimed. "You must be baking something?" Her voice carried an inflection that made it more a question than a statement.

Lucy nodded. "There's a casserole in the oven for dinner," she said. "I'm not very good at that kind of thing yet. Before I was married, I never did interest myself in cooking and baking as some of my sisters did."

Lavina chuckled as she shrugged out of her coat. "I understand," she said. "I'm only learning to enjoy cooking myself. Where should I hang my coat?"

"Over here, behind the stove," Lucy said, motioning. Then she tensed herself. *Now it'll start,* she thought. *Now she'll start telling me all about everything that's different from the way she had it. And when she does, I'll . . .*

However, she never got the chance to find out. When Lavina turned from the hooks on the wall, she noticed the flowering geraniums on the windowsill. A few quick steps took her to the window. "Oh, how do you get these to bloom in the wintertime?" Lavina asked as she stroked the dainty petals. "Somehow, mine never do very well when I have them in the house."

Now this is different. Lavina Zook, the "perfect

housekeeper" asking me, Lucy Weaver, for advice. Lucy hardly knew what to make of it. She rubbed her hands together, trying hard to think fast. "Well," she began finally, "I think they like a lot of sunshine, so I try to have them in the south windows."

"And you have such nice, big south windows in this house," Lavina added. "With such a good view across the fields to the woods over there."

"Yes," Lucy agreed. Together they stood and looked out the window, watching the raindrops splash in the puddles outside. Lucy stole a glance at the lady beside her. *What will we talk about for another two whole hours until dinnertime?* Since this visitor had turned out so differently than she had expected, Lucy felt strangely lost.

"Oh," Lavina said suddenly. "Here come Larry and the boys toward the garage. Larry promised to show the boys the footprints in there, and they wouldn't let him forget it."

"The footprints?" Lucy asked, astonished and horrified. *How does this man know what is in our garage? Does he really expect to show his boys some muddy footprints?*

"Yes, the footprints," Lavina answered matter-of-factly. "Let's join them. I haven't seen them either for quite a while." She turned to walk across the kitchen.

A thousand thoughts flew through Lucy's mind before she reached the door. She could not imagine what this strange man would want with the footprints in her garage. Apparently they had been there for quite a while. *Where can they be? How is it that I never noticed them if they are so outstanding?"* With a sigh, she opened the door from the kitchen to the garage as the men entered the garage through the outside door. Joel caught her eye, and Lucy could see that he was nearly as puzzled as she was.

Larry smiled into Lucy's flustered face. "So you haven't seen the footprints either?" Larry chuckled. "Your husband declares there are none here, and I decided to enlighten him." He glanced around. "Oh, I see you've put a cupboard on top of them. Is it all right to move the cupboard a little?"

Joel and Larry pulled the cupboard from the corner. "And you covered them with a board yet!" Larry exclaimed. "Didn't you like them, or what?"

Joel scratched his head. "I remember now," he said. "When we put the cupboard there, Mother said the floor was uneven. She put that board down to keep the cupboard from rocking. The cupboard has been here longer than you have, Lucy, and I don't suppose you ever went looking underneath here, did you?"

Lucy shook her head.

The four Zook boys crowded around the patch of exposed concrete, and Lucy bent over them to see what they were examining. Sure enough, there in the corner, were four sets of small footprints imprinted in the concrete. Beside them, several indistinct marks looked as if someone had tried to smooth out something there while the concrete was still soft.

"Father, which are mine?" the biggest boy asked. "Those?"

"Yes, yours are the biggest ones," Larry agreed. "Do you remember the lesson I said you should remember about those footprints, when we made them?"

Lucy straightened herself quickly. *So these footprints hold a lesson yet! What will I find out next?*

"Something about habits, right?" This came from the second-biggest boy.

"That's right." Larry squatted beside the footprints and pulled his daughter onto his knee. With his finger, he traced the largest and clearest set of footprints. "Can you change these footprints?" he asked the boys clustered around him.

"No, of course not, Father."

"You're right," Larry agreed. "Apart from destroying the concrete, these footprints are here to stay. Over here"—and he traced around the faint, shallow marks on the floor—"we made some footprints with the baby's feet. That was you," he said, hugging the small girl on his lap. "Those tracks were small, and I could easily wipe them out with my hand, right after we made them. These tracks"—and he indicated the biggest ones again— "are big and deep. We left them in the concrete too long, and now they are there to stay." He pointed to the two sets of footprints between the smallest and the largest ones. "These I left for several hours before I tried to wipe them out, and these I left for one day. As you can see, they still left their marks, even after I tried to smooth them over."

Lucy listened intently. Larry had a way of making his words sound gentle and yet deep. But what kind of sermon could come out of footprints in the concrete?

She did not wait long to find out. Larry looked around at his little audience and cleared his throat. "When we are young," he began, "our lives are like soft concrete. We can make any mark on them that we want to, and it makes an impression." He stopped and smiled at the thoughtful faces of his sons.

"These footprints are like our habits," he went on. "It doesn't matter whether they're good habits or bad habits. It is easy to start a habit and make marks on our lives. If we wipe them out right away, then they come away clean and we can hardly see them anymore. But if we let them stay for a little while, it becomes harder and harder to get rid of them. As we become older, the concrete starts to set. If we let the marks stay for a while, it becomes almost impossible to get them out. The ones we don't do anything about are here to stay, short of destroying the concrete, or our lives. So it is good to be careful what kind of habits we allow ourselves to have. Eventually the concrete sets, and no one but God can help us take the marks out."

Larry cleared his throat and continued, "Many years ago, a wise man said, 'First we form our habits; then our habits form us. Conquer your bad habits, or they'll eventually conquer you.' "

Lucy squirmed. Suddenly her habit of worrying over things loomed up dark and terrible. Larry's explanation was so fitting. *I'll do something about it today yet,* she vowed to herself.

"That's really something," Joel commented when he and Larry had set the cupboard into its place again. "Thank you for showing us the footprints and for telling us what they meant. Now, you're going to stay for dinner, right?"

"You're welcome," Larry answered. "And, yes"—his eyes twinkled—"we had hoped we could stay for dinner if it's not too much bother for you."

Everyone looked at Lucy, who swallowed bravely. "Of course you'll stay for dinner," she stated quietly. "I feel we owe you at least that much for what you've told us today." Although she did not explain what she meant, she could see that Joel understood.

Several hours later, Joel and Lucy stood together on the front steps and watched their visitors disappear around the bend. "Well," Joel began when Lucy made no comment, "can we think of something else now besides polishing the place for the 'perfect housekeeper' to inspect?"

As Lucy turned to go inside, she smiled into Joel's twinkling eyes. "Actually," she admitted, "I feel a little foolish for being so worried about her. I found her an understanding friend. Why, she barely looked around at all, except at the garage floor. And that happened to be one place I hadn't cleaned yet."

Joel followed her through the door. "Does that mean all your cleaning was in vain?" he wondered.

"Not exactly," Lucy told him. "This way I have a head start on my housecleaning. But I don't feel like telling anyone about all the cleaning I've done, since my worries all came to nothing."

"That's how worries always are," Joel explained. "So we never really get anywhere by getting all worked up about things."

"That I'm finding out," Lucy answered. Then her eyes smiled into his. "Do you know what I'd

like to do in the garage?" she asked. "You'd better like it because you're going to have to help."

"Oh, no!" Joel cowered in mock fear. "I hope
you don't plan to houseclean that yet today! You've
done enough cleaning around here in the past
week to last all year, I'm sure."

Lucy ignored his remark. "I want to move that
cupboard into the other corner, beside the door.
That way I can see those footprints in the concrete every time I hang up the wash. Maybe that
will help me to remember about habits and what
they do to us." She stopped, amazed at the look
on Joel's face. "Surely you don't think it's too
late for me to stop worrying, do you?" she asked
anxiously.

"No, of course not." Joel's voice was husky. "God
and I will help you all we can. And if you're ready
to try to overcome it, you've taken the biggest step
already. Let's move that cupboard right now. Maybe
it will help us to remember that habits are more
permanent than we'd like to think."

Lucy paused with her hand on the doorknob.
"Yes," she agreed softly. "But I'm glad that with
God all things are possible, and that He is able to
help us overcome our habits. I'm certainly going
to need His help with mine."

9

A Good Place

" 'Lead me to some soul today,' " nineteen-year-old Brent sang to himself as he shifted his father's cube van smoothly through its gears. " 'Teach me, Lord, just what to say . . .' " Driving toward the pink, early-morning sky, he glanced at his youngest brother, Arnold, sitting beside him with all the importance of his four years. Arnold did not often go along to town, so when he did, he felt very grown-up.

Brent enjoyed these weekly pickup and delivery trips to town. In the Witmers' out-of-the-way community, nearly everyone knew everyone else. And since the nearest town was almost an hour's drive away, the Witmers had developed this once-a-week delivery schedule to bring their farm products to the town customers who desired them.

Today, however, Brent had no vegetables for sale. The snowbanks beside the road reminded him that it was still January. Today he had Arnold to take care of. Arnold was the last child of a large family, and he was used to wearing his brothers' hand-me-downs. But this winter, he had rapidly outgrown all the available boots. Father's eyes had twinkled when Arnold announced one morning that no one had outgrown boots for him to borrow anymore.

"Are we almost there?" Arnold asked, breaking into Brent's thoughts. "I'm cold. Can you turn on the heater?"

"Yes, of course," Brent answered, reaching for the dial. "And, no, we're not there yet. You'll have time to get good and warm before we reach Cobourg."

"Oh," said Arnold, still shivering. "Where all are we going today?"

"First I must deliver Mrs. Humphrey's ten dozen eggs," Brent told him. "Then Annie Morphet wanted some sausage, and Herman Goodfunk ordered cheese. I must pick up the groceries for Mother and not forget to check whether the boots we ordered for Arnold have come in." He grinned at Arnold. "And, of course, all the regular customers will be waiting for their bread and rolls. But first of all, I hope we reach the gas station just outside of town before this thing runs out of gas."

"We will," Arnold stated. Then he looked a bit worried. "I hope so anyway."

Brent did not reply. He did not like the looks of the fuel gauge, but he could do nothing about it. Houses were few and far between in this area, and gas stations even more so. He knew that there were only two between home and Cobourg, and the gas can that he usually carried had been emptied only yesterday. "Keep us, Father," he prayed. "If it be Your will, please keep us from running out."

Not many miles later, the truck sputtered and coughed. "It can't be!" Brent groaned. "Still three miles from the gas station." He tried to stay calm as he steered the truck to a stop on the shoulder of the road.

Arnold turned away from the window, surprise written on his face. "What are you doing?" he wanted to know. "Can't we go anymore?"

"No, we can't," Brent answered. "And here we sit." He looked at Arnold thoughtfully.

"Are we going to have to walk?" Arnold wondered. His eyes grew big at the thought.

Brent shook his head. "Three miles would be a long walk for a little fellow like you. Especially when it's so cold. And I hate to think of leaving you here alone."

Further, he thought to himself, *I don't want to leave the load in the back of my truck unattended for so long.*

"So I guess"—he looked at Arnold—" we'll just have to sit and see who comes along."

Almost as soon as he had said that, Brent noticed a pair of headlights pulling to a stop behind his truck. He watched in the mirror as a stocky figure jumped out of the pickup and bustled up beside him. "Need any help?" the young man asked. "Can I do something for you?"

"Why, Seth Hansen!" Brent answered. "Yes, you can. I've run out of gas. I have a can along; could you possibly fill it up for me?"

Seth grinned. "Sure," he said. "Of course. Be glad to help. Is the can in the back, did you say?"

"Yes, it is," Brent said. "Let me get it for you."

Before very long, the friendly young man in the pickup was back again. Without ceremony, he grabbed the now-full gas can and poured gas into Brent's tank.

Brent climbed out of the cab and joined him. "I really appreciate your helping me like this," he began. "How much do I owe you for your trouble?"

Seth shook his head. "You don't owe me anything," he said. "I'm glad to help. But maybe you can do something for me."

Brent blinked. "Perhaps," he said.

Seth rubbed his hand over his eyes, in seeming indecision. Then he blurted out quickly, "I know you and your friends are good people, Brent. And I'm wondering if you could pray for me." He watched Brent's face almost pleadingly.

"Why, of course we could pray for you," Brent answered. "What should we pray for?"

By now the gas can had gurgled itself empty, so the two young men moved behind the truck. "It's like this," Seth began. "I'm on my way just now to apply for an opening at Confederation Tech School. They have a program for training truck drivers. Then they help the successful ones find jobs, you know."

Brent nodded.

"Well," said Seth, "I really need a good place to work. I need to support my mother now, since her insurance ran out. And"—he smiled shyly—"I'd like to get married soon. So I really need a job. Could you pray that I'll graduate from the school and find a local job?"

Brent thought a bit, and then he nodded. "Why sure, Seth, I think we can do that."

Seth sighed just a little and shook Brent's hand heartily. "That's wonderful. Thanks a lot. It makes me feel better already. So long now." And he jumped into his pickup.

As Brent slid into the truck, he met Arnold's wondering eyes. "Who was that?" Arnold wanted to know.

"That was Seth Hansen," Brent explained. "Remember the old lady who lives down the road from Grandpa's? Seth is her son, and he lives by himself in the little pink house at the end of the street in Piney."

Arnold nodded.

Brent started the truck, and then he looked at Arnold. "Seth wants us to pray for him," he told Arnold. "Let's bow our heads right now and pray before we start driving again."

During the next few weeks, Brent often thought about Seth's request. After he told his parents about his encounter on the highway, the whole family prayed regularly for Seth. It became a fascinating assignment to them, and they often wondered about the results of their prayers.

Some weeks later, the Witmers were interrupted at the supper table by the rumble of the feed truck coming in the lane. Father nodded to Brent and fifteen-year-old Jason to help unload the feed. "I only ordered three tons this time," Father called after them. "So it shouldn't take long to unload."

Brent stamped into his boots and hurried after Jason. When he reached the truck, he stopped in surprise. The truck driver had swung down from his cab and stood grinning in front of the two young men. He looked immensely pleased with himself.

"Seth Hansen!" Brent exclaimed at last. "Where did you come from? Aren't you still in tech school?"

"Nope," Seth answered. "I graduated from the course last week, and I found a place to work right away, and here I am." He stuck out his hand and pumped Brent's hand up and down. "And I'd like to thank you folks for your prayers. I'm sure they helped me a lot. I really appreciate that."

"You're very welcome," Brent answered. "It was no problem for us. But"—he looked steadily into Seth's eyes—"we're going to keep on praying for your soul. We want you to find a place in God's kingdom as well. Do you know what I mean?"

Seth shifted and suddenly seemed uncomfortable. "I guess I do. Your prayers work; I've seen that for myself. So I don't mind if you keep on praying. But for right now, let's unload this feed, shall we?"

"Yes," said Brent. "But don't forget that a place in God's kingdom is a lot more important than a place to work. Make sure you find that place before it's too late."

10

Disaster Ahead

Never in all of his nineteen years had Jerry heard such an impassioned speech. Even now, he stood looking at neighbor Dennis and tried to make sense of the torrent of words that he had just heard. Dennis, still agitated, shifted from one foot to the other, waiting for a response from Jerry.

"Well," Jerry said finally, "I promise we'll think about it. I doubt if my father will do much about it though."

Dennis nearly jumped up and down. "Do more than think about it," he demanded. "Please! Do everything you can to get ready. Tomorrow I'm going to town to order my wood stove. Shall I order one for you too?"

Jerry shook his head. "No. If we need one, we'll order one ourselves, I'm sure."

Dennis frowned as he climbed into his pickup truck. "Now you can't say I didn't warn you," he said, shaking his forefinger at Jerry. "Don't let that day catch you unprepared." He left the farmyard, spitting gravel with his tires as he went.

Jerry watched him go; then he turned to enter the barn, where Father and his younger sister had started the evening milking.

Father looked up from washing cows as Jerry passed by. "So, what did our neighbor want today?" he asked. "He seemed to have a lot of important things to say to you."

"He did," Jerry answered. "He said that he wanted to talk to me, since you wouldn't believe him anyhow. And I think I know why he said that." Jerry paused to pick up a fork for feeding the cows. "But I'm still troubled by what Dennis had to say," he confessed.

"And what was that?" Father asked pointedly.

"About . . . well, about the future," Jerry answered. "We seem to hear more and more about this lately. Dennis gave some pretty strong warnings about what will happen when the computers stop running and there'll be no electricity. He showed me his pickup load. Father, you should have seen it. He had his pickup loaded full with bulk foods in bags and boxes. He intends to keep collecting food until he has two and a half tons of dried food in his basement. Then he will guard it with a shotgun when it comes closer to the time he expects things to happen. He said we should make a stockpile too, and he even offered to guard it for us."

Father smiled but said nothing.

"And then," Jerry went on, "he wanted to know what will happen with our cows when we no longer have electricity to milk them. I pointed out that we milk by generator once a month, just to make sure that everything works. And though it often seems that the electricity goes off at the most inconvenient times, we've gotten along so far."

Father nodded and plugged in another milker. "That was a good answer," he said. "Was that everything he said?"

Jerry had been forking silage from the feed cart as he talked. He pushed the cart around the corner and positioned it so that he could feed the next batch of cows. "No, that wasn't everything," he answered. "Next he wanted to know what will happen when all the electric fences in the country don't work anymore, and there are cows all over the place. He made it sound quite serious."

Jerry stopped to unplug a water bowl. And then Susanna's voice came from beside a cow.

"Doesn't Dennis know about solar-powered fencers? Hasn't he ever seen our solar panels out there by the gate?"

"Apparently not before today." Jerry smiled at her. "He got all excited when I pointed them out, and he said that he'll need to buy some and give them to his brother-in-law. He also said that tomorrow he's going to order a wood stove for his house, and he offered to order one for us. He thought we needed one badly, but I didn't tell him that we already have a wood-burning furnace in our basement."

Susanna chuckled. "He's lived beside us for almost six years now, and he still didn't notice that? What kind of neighbor is he?"

"A fearful one, I believe," Jerry answered as he pushed his cart farther down the aisle. He started whistling a tune, and Susanna joined in with her clear alto. " 'God will take care of you, / Through every day, / O'er all the way; / He will take care of you . . .' "

Later, at the supper table, Mother opened the subject again by asking Jerry, "Did Dennis have something on his mind today? He certainly detained you long enough on your way to the barn."

"That he did," Jerry agreed. "And he certainly had something on his mind." Then Jerry proceeded to explain all the dire predictions that he had heard from their neighbor. As he talked, he noticed that Susanna was appearing more and more serious and that her eyes became larger and larger. So he concluded his speech with "What do you think, Father? Is it time that we get excited about this problem?"

Susanna set down her water glass. "But there could be something to it," she blurted out. "If so many people are so afraid, surely they know something about what's coming. Shouldn't we at least do something to get ready in case some of those things come true?"

Father shook his head slowly. "Fear is never a good reaction," he said. "Fear makes people irrational, and they do all sorts of things they wouldn't otherwise do. In the Book of Revelation, God puts fearful people into the same class as unbelievers and murderers and immoral people."

Susanna looked deep in thought. "I guess that would apply here, wouldn't it."

"Indeed it does," Father told her. "And did you forget about all the preparations we have made already for such a time?"

"What do you mean?" Susanna asked. "I never caught on that we were doing that."

"Not likely," Father answered. "Because we do so many of these things anyway. We are very blessed here on the farm. Every year we put away our garden produce. We bake our own bread, and we already heat our house with our wood-burning furnace. We could possibly make a few more preparations, but if disaster should come, I feel that we are as well prepared as we need to be."

Susanna looked thoughtful. "So you think disaster might come?"

"It might," Father admitted. "Although absolutely no one knows just to what extent. I really believe that North America is ripe for some kind of judgment. I recently discovered that four times the Bible talks about God laughing at the heathen. In Proverbs, God actually says to the wicked, 'I will laugh at your calamity.' This problem with the computers could be just such a calamity that God would laugh at. Computers are quite an invention, true. But they came about only because men learned to harness the laws that God had already put into place. For many years, people thought they were getting smarter and smarter and that eventually they would use computers to rule the world. In many cases, I believe, men are worshiping the computer and its power instead of God. I wouldn't be surprised if God would allow computers to bring men to their knees so that He can show them that He is still 'King of kings, and Lord of lords,' as He has said."

Jerry nodded in agreement, and Mother smiled

at Susanna. "In the Psalms we read David's testimony. 'I have been young, and now am old,' " Mother quoted quietly, " 'yet have I not seen the righteous forsaken, nor his seed begging bread.' What a wonderful promise!"

"That's true," Father agreed. "And now just one more thing. So many people are looking into the future and becoming afraid, and they forget about the many times we are admonished to be ready for the Lord's return. That is at least certain, while this other disaster is anyone's guess. Who knows? Christ may return before the other disaster strikes. Then all the current fears will come to nothing and be replaced with a much greater fear in the hearts of unbelievers. Thousands of people are feverishly preparing for an uncertain disaster. But how many are preparing themselves for the sure return of the Lord?"

"Not very many, by the looks of things," Jerry answered.

"Not enough," Mother said soberly.

"So let's be sure that we are prepared for the great Day of the Lord," Father concluded. "As for this unknown disaster, we will do what we can and trust God with the rest, since He alone knows the outcome of all things."

"That's right," said Mother.

Jerry and Susanna echoed, "That's right."

11

God and the Traffic Jam

"Yes, but how do you know it's God taking care of you and not just your own intelligence looking out for yourself?" Brett asked. "Fiddlesticks, all this talk about how God takes care of people. It does not make much sense to me."

Alvin sighed and closed the ledger on his desk. "No, my dear cousin," he said, "I don't suppose it will make sense to you as long as you don't really believe in God's love for you."

Brett shrugged. "Maybe not. It seems to make sense to you, so I guess that's all that matters for now."

Alvin looked deep into his cousin's dark, troubled eyes and sighed again. So many times in the last three days, he had felt especially burdened about Brett's seeming indifference to the teachings that Alvin held dear. What had gone wrong? As children, they had spent many happy hours together. Alvin clearly remembered the deep convictions that Uncle Dwayne had spoken of. But that was before Uncle Dwayne had moved to Montana. In the nine years since, Alvin had seen very little of the family. Until now, at least. Now his cousin Brett had come back to southern Ontario for an extended visit. While the two spent time together at the family manufacturing business, Alvin suddenly found out just how far apart he and his cousin were in the things that mattered.

Alvin shook his head as if to clear it of such gloomy thoughts. "I've got to go to London now," he said, "to pick up those lock parts at the plater's. Care to come along?"

"Might as well," Brett answered, grinning. "I'm just getting into everybody's way here in the shop."

"Oh, no," Alvin objected. "We're happy to have you here. But you might need a break." He picked up the keys from the rack beside his desk and led the way outside.

The two boys chatted pleasantly as they drove through the autumn countryside. Alvin found, to his surprise, that Brett still remembered many of the landmarks as they passed them. "But how do you do it?" he asked finally. "I'm surprised you remember so many things from when you were only ten years old."

"Oh, I remember things easily," Brett answered lightly. "And you and my father have talked about many things already too."

"Could be," Alvin replied. "Just be careful to use your memory for the proper things." He brought the pickup to a smooth halt at a traffic light on the outskirts of the city. Then he glanced at Brett. "Which way should we go around the business section?" he asked. "I don't care to get tied up in traffic this time of day."

"Go right," Brett said, motioning in that direction. "I wouldn't mind seeing the Clavate plant again, where my father worked for a while."

"River Road it shall be then," Alvin agreed, "even if this way is a few minutes longer than the other way."

"I don't mind," Brett said, grinning.

"I don't either," Alvin said, grinning back. "Father said I should be back before quitting time; otherwise, he doesn't mind if I take you around a bit."

Brett settled back in his seat. "I enjoy being with you," he admitted. "You seem so . . . well, so solid or settled or something."

"Help me to witness to him of Your love, Father," Alvin prayed silently. "Don't let him go home again with all of his unanswered questions still unanswered."

Before Alvin could think of anything to say, Brett sat up suddenly. "Hey, don't tell me Clavate isn't any farther than this! It used to be a terribly long ways out here!"

"You've grown up a lot between ten and nineteen," Alvin told him. "Things get smaller when you grow up, even distances." And both boys chuckled as Brett craned his neck to see every bit of the sprawling plant as they went by.

"Here we are at Scandic Metal Finishing," Alvin announced nearly fifteen minutes later. "Come along inside. I'd like to introduce you to James." Obediently, Brett uncoiled his long legs and followed Alvin into the building.

Once inside, however, Alvin forgot all about introducing his cousin. James gave Alvin one look and gasped in surprise. "Alvin!" he exclaimed. "Where did you come from? Didn't you know that Highbury Avenue is closed? Our driver just radioed back that he's stuck in traffic—a gasoline tanker rammed into the overpass at Wellington Street and exploded. Made a big mess, sure did. Traffic's piled up in every direction, and at least three people were killed."

"We came around the other way," Alvin explained.

"Well, you're two very lucky boys," James declared, shaking his head. "It happened only four minutes ago, and it usually takes about that long to get from here to that corner."

Alvin shook his head. "Not lucky, James," he said. "That was God taking care of us."

"I don't see how He did it," James answered, still shaking his head. "I didn't expect to see you for quite a while with all that mess on the road. But here are your parts now; can you sign for them here?"

Alvin picked up the pen James offered him, and signed his name to the packing slip on the desk. Then he picked up the box of shiny silver parts and stepped through the swinging doors into the sunshine outdoors. He plunked the heavy box into the pickup bed and hopped into the driver's seat. Only then did he dare to look at Brett again.

"Well, Brett," he asked, choosing his words carefully, "are you going to tell me it was your own intelligence that picked River Road instead of Highbury Avenue?"

"It sure wasn't," Brett readily agreed. "I had no way of knowing what would happen on the other road."

"That was God taking care of us." Alvin

watched Brett carefully as he said it. He saw Brett's eyes widen and a look of understanding come over his face.

Then Brett turned and looked Alvin full in the face. "I'm convinced of that now," he said simply.

12

Helping Out

"Good evening, Ethel," Maria greeted the sister beside her after prayer meeting. Then, knowing the young mother's struggles, she asked, "Have you heard from your husband lately?"

Ethel looked troubled. "Not really," she replied. "At least not directly. You know that the judge ordered him to keep on paying the rent on our house?"

Maria nodded. "And does he?"

"No," Ethel replied. "He apparently told our landlord last week that he cannot do that. And I am not earning enough with my sewing to handle such a high rent besides supporting myself and our three children. So I found out today that I have until the end of next week; then I'll need to get out of the house. And I don't know what to do." The last sentence sounded more like a wail than a statement.

"Well," Maria answered slowly, "I'm sure the Lord has something in mind for you. My husband is the deacon here, you know. So I'll mention it to him and see what he says. Remember, Ethel, we are all brothers and sisters, and we'll see that you have a place to live. Somehow, I'm sure, God will provide."

"Oh, I thank you!" Ethel exclaimed. "That makes me feel better already." She squeezed Maria's hand gratefully.

Then she turned and gathered up her sleeping baby. "Come, Joshua. It's time we start on our sixty-minute drive home."

Later, as Maria and her husband drove home, Maria told him what Ethel had said. "She really does need a place to live if that house is no longer available to her," Maria ended. "We know that she gets almost no support at all from her husband since the last time he left her. And I know she'd like to live closer to the rest of us here, now that she has become a member of our congregation."

Kevin nodded without replying. Then he rubbed his face and scratched his head. Finally he said, "You know what? Brother Isaac told me just this evening that his tenant house will be empty again the beginning of next week. He's looking for someone to live there."

Maria blinked several times. "Really?" she exclaimed. "How does that happen?"

"Well, you know they had that older couple living in there for several years. Now their children have arranged for them to go and live with their son in Arizona, which will be a good idea all around, I'm sure. But to learn about that right now—when Ethel and her children need a place to stay—is amazing. I think I will call Brother Isaac when we get home and see what he says."

That telephone call turned into more telephone calls. Brother Isaac readily consented to let Ethel Voth and her children live in his tenant house at a very reasonable rent. Kevin and Maria relayed that information to Ethel. And she agreed not to pursue her husband through the courts to continue paying the rent.

Just before Kevin and Maria dropped off to sleep, Ethel called them back. "I'm so grateful to you," she said. "I just know that I'll be able to sleep much better tonight, knowing what I know now."

"Oh, you're welcome," Maria assured her. "That's what a brotherhood is for."

"Well, I don't know how I can ever thank you enough. But good night for now."

"Good night," Maria replied.

Two days later, Ethel telephoned again. "I'm so sorry," she began. "Next Saturday will have to be my last day here. So it looks as if Brother Isaac's tenant house will be just right for me. But I can't possibly get my stuff all packed and moved in one week's time, besides doing the two large orders of sewing that I have."

"Oh, Ethel," Maria replied, "I'm so glad you're telling me your needs. I've talked to several of the sisters at church, and we're going to come and help you every day next week. And our husbands will be ready to help you move on Saturday."

With tears in her voice, Ethel replied, "Really? Really and truly? You'll actually come and help a single mother move?"

"Why, yes, of course," Maria assured her. "A brotherhood is for helping each other."

So that was how it came about that for a whole week two sisters made the hour drive every day to help Ethel get ready for the moving day. When Saturday came, nearly every truck and van in the congregation made the trip in one long convoy. When Ethel saw them coming, she gasped and grabbed the doorpost. "How can you do all this for me?" she cried. "I never expected this. I can't possibly pay you all."

"Don't worry about that," Kevin told her.

"What should we load first? Oh, and by the way, my wife is arranging lunch for this whole crew."

In a daze, Ethel watched the men as they carried her furniture and belongings out of her house by every available exit. In less time than she could have imagined, her house was empty, and she and her children were following the convoy down the road. And in a surprisingly short time, they had arranged her furniture in the cozy little house behind the barn on Brother Isaac's farm. Just before suppertime, someone even washed the floor.

As her friend Maria stood in the doorway, surveying the work of the day, Ethel approached her again. "Something still bothers me," she said. "I don't know how I can possibly pay everyone who helped me today. This is the easiest moving day I ever heard about, and I want to show my appreciation to all of you. Why, some of the men worked from morning till evening."

Maria chuckled. "We don't want any pay," she said. "All of us understood that we were volunteering our time today."

"Even the dinner that you brought in for all these helpers?" Ethel asked. "And the leftovers that you so kindly gave to me?"

"Even the dinner," Maria assured her.

Ethel's face lit up, and a long sigh escaped her. "I think I understand," she said. "And as I said,

I'm truly grateful to all of you. And if any of you ever decide to move, just let me know, and I'll be there to help."

Maria's face beamed. "You've caught the idea," she praised. "It's the love of God at work in our hearts. Today we helped you, and another day someone else might need help. Didn't I ever tell you that a brotherhood is for helping each other?"

"Yes, you did," Ethel replied. "But I never understood how the love of God could be so practical. I'm glad I'm part of a brotherhood like this!"

"So am I," Maria agreed with a smile. "And may God bless you in your new home!"

13

Hospitality

"No, Peter, I cannot do that," Diane said, and her voice carried finality. She jabbed her crochet hook into the doily she was making as if it were the most important thing in the world.

Even from across the room, Peter looked surprised. "Why not, Diane?" he asked.

"You know I can't cook very well, Peter. And you know that I simply dread the thought of cooking for company."

Peter laid his pen on the desk, crossed the room, and sat beside her on the sofa. "Now, Diane, we've gone through this before," he began gently. "You know I like your cooking. If I like it, there is a good chance others will too. And there is nothing wrong with serving a simple meal to visitors. I think that is better than stuffing people with huge, fancy dinners.

"Besides, the Bible tells us to use hospitality without grudging. I don't see how we can do that when you don't want to cook."

Diane made several stitches in silence. Yes, she knew very well how Peter felt about having visitors. Ever since their wedding four months before, he had wanted to invite several of their married friends for a meal. Tonight, for some reason, he persisted even after she had told him again that the idea did not interest her at all.

Diane looked at her cozy surroundings. Deep within herself, she shuddered at the thought of children—someone else's children—spilling the toys all over the floor and tracking mud over her soft, spotless carpet. And someone would surely spill ashes from the fireplace and mar her beautiful, polished hearth.

Peter's voice brought her back to the present. "You'll have to start inviting people sometime," he was telling her. "You don't intend to be a recluse the rest of your life, do you?"

Diane shook her head. "Not really."

As if sensing her thoughts, Peter went on. "I know you've worked hard to get this old house into such good shape. But don't you think we're a little bit selfish, or maybe proud, if we refuse to share it with others for fear they will spoil it?"

"Maybe you're right," Diane reluctantly agreed.

Peter's face brightened. "Then, since we'll have to start sometime, and no time is better than the present, may I invite Jesse and Carol for Sunday dinner?"

Diane smiled at his enthusiasm. Although she did not share his eagerness, she found herself slowly nodding her head. Still, somehow, she could not forget that Jesse and Carol had two-year-old twins.

"That's my good little wife," Peter praised her. "I'm sure you won't be sorry for this."

As Diane watched him stride toward the telephone, she told herself grimly, *It's all right for him to be eager; he doesn't have the dinner to make and the house to clean up all in one day's time.*

The next day, Diane remembered Peter's advice about a simple meal for visitors. But she seemed to have trouble following it. *After all,* she told herself while she washed the breakfast dishes, *Mother always said you can't have Sunday dinner without a roast. This time all we have is a chicken, so I guess it'll have to do. And we'll need at least one salad, besides a hot vegetable and mashed potatoes. Then we'll need fresh bread, and a cake, and some pudding. Oh, and I mustn't forget to make strawberry pie to eat with ice cream. Carol makes such delicious dinners, and I must not let her think I can't cook as well as she can.*

Let's see, she went on. *I'll finish my cleaning first. That should give me at least half a day to do the cooking.* Already the day's work loomed large before her.

A little doubtfully, Diane thought over the list again. Would she have time to do all of that? *But I must,* she decided, *or my mother would say I didn't even serve a real company meal. Besides, I've promised Peter we could have company for tomorrow, and I can't back out on him now.*

All morning, Diane scrubbed and polished. She even cleaned the bedroom carpet as though it had not been cleaned before. When Peter came in for dinner, she still had the kitchen floor to wash.

"Oh, come on," Peter said gently. "Do you have to wash that floor every week, when just the two of us walk on it? It surely doesn't look dirty to me."

"But it is," Diane insisted. "My mother always said that a kitchen floor must be washed every week or you're not done with your cleaning."

"Can't you leave it, just for this once?" Peter asked. "I know you're tired from working hard all morning. Why don't you take a nap after dinner instead of scrubbing this floor?"

"I can't," returned Diane sharply. "I still have

all the cooking to do for tomorrow. And there is not a thing ready for lunch now, and it's five minutes after twelve." She swished past Peter with her bucket of water and went to empty it. When she came back into the kitchen, Peter had set a pot on the stove and was pouring a can of soup into it to heat.

Feeling ashamed of her sharp words, Diane silently gathered bowls and silverware and set the table. Then she sliced bread and cheese and brought the rest of a banana pie from the refrigerator. Meanwhile, Peter kept on stirring the soup and staring into the pot.

After they were seated, Peter asked the blessing and then dished soup into his bowl. Diane silently buttered her slice of bread, wondering what Peter would say. She knew that she had hurt him, but somehow she could not bring herself to apologize. Throughout that silent meal, Diane agonized over it. When they had finished eating, she still had not said a word.

Peter pushed his chair back and cleared his throat. "I'll be working at my desk for several hours this afternoon. If you need help with anything, just call me." His voice sounded strangely strained.

"Okay. I probably won't need much help though," Diane told him.

Hospitality

When Peter was out of sight, Diane jumped up quickly. *I'll leave the dinner dishes,* she decided. *That way, I can scrub this floor right away and maybe wax it yet too. Then I can look for a cake recipe while it dries.*

Suiting action to thought, she gathered her aluminum scrub bucket and the soap. Then she knelt in one corner, ready to start washing the floor. She surveyed the distance between herself and the other end of the kitchen, and it seemed like a large task to scrub that entire floor. Peter's question echoed in her mind: "Can't you leave it, just this once?" *No,* she told herself firmly as she wrung out the cloth, *I absolutely can't do that this time. Carol will surely notice if I leave it dirty.*

As she worked, Diane reflected on the events of the evening before. She remembered other times when she had resisted Peter's suggestion to invite company. She had always persuaded him that she was not ready for it yet. *Why is it,* she asked herself, *that I find it so hard to submit to Peter in this matter?*

A small whisper started within her. It gnawed insistently at her conscience until Diane sat back on her heels to listen to it. "A lover of hospitality." "Use hospitality one to another without grudging." "Wives, submit yourselves." "Young women to be . . . obedient to their own husbands."

Diane bowed her head. *I haven't been doing that,* she had to admit. She sat quietly for several minutes, pondering those verses. At last she sighed deeply. *I give up,* she said to herself. *I can't enjoy peace anyway. At least not while I'm resisting in my heart what Peter wants to do.*

She resumed washing the floor. But the small whisper did not stop. "A man's pride shall bring him low," it went on relentlessly.

Diane sighed again. "Lord," she whispered, "I'm tired of this turmoil. And I'm sorry for being proud of my house, and for not supporting Peter's suggestions about inviting company. Please help me to correct my attitudes. And please help me to make this right with Peter."

Diane took a deep breath. Not for a long time had she felt so free. *Why, I feel as if a load rolled off my back,* she realized suddenly. *My pride was becoming a bigger problem than I realized. I'm sure Peter must have sensed the root of my problem . . .* She looked at the door to the living room and then at the small patch of floor that still needed scrubbing.

As soon as I finish this floor, she decided, *I will tell him all about it. He will be pleased to know I've changed my mind.* In happy anticipation, Diane tackled the rest of the floor.

A little later, she straightened her back and

sighed. "There, I'm finished," she announced to herself. She braced herself on her bucket to get up. Just then, her wet hands slipped on the rim, and both hands landed forcefully on the floor.

"Oh, how could I be so clumsy?" Diane groaned. Already an angry welt ran up her left arm. As it started to bleed, she hurried to the bathroom before any blood spots could stain her clean floor.

Hearing her, Peter came quickly to see what had happened. "Are you all right?" he asked, concern written on his face.

"Yes, I think I am," Diane assured him. "But my arm is sore."

Peter examined it carefully. "It's just a bad scratch from the handle of the bucket," he declared. "But you'd better bandage it, or it might become infected. Here, let me help you wrap it up."

"But I can't finish my work with a bandaged hand," she protested.

"We won't bandage it all the way," Peter assured her. "See, the bandage will only reach to your wrist. Then all you'll need to do is keep it from getting wet for a day or so."

Diane's eyes were still doubtful when Peter had finished wrapping her arm. "This way I can't make bread anymore today," she said. "And I didn't even start with all the rest of the cooking I wanted to do."

Peter followed her as she walked to the kitchen and picked up a recipe book. "Should I tell Jesse that it doesn't suit for them to come tomorrow?" he asked. "I'm sure they would understand."

Diane thought about that for a minute. "No," she said finally, "it will never be easy to invite company again if we back out this time. And by tomorrow morning, my arm will feel much better than it does now."

Then she took a deep breath and plunged into what she wanted to say. She told Peter all about the struggle with her self, and the victory she had won while washing the floor. "I'm sorry, Peter, for the way I haven't cooperated with you about this," she finished. "It was only my selfishness that said I didn't like to cook for company. I was afraid I couldn't serve a grand enough meal. I was also proud of our house, and that is why I insisted that it must be shiny and spotless before we could have visitors. Can you forgive me for being so quarrelsome?"

Peter's voice was husky as he answered, "I forgive you, Diane. From now on, let's work together on our problems. For a starter, how can I help you with the things you need to do yet this afternoon?"

"I can make a cake with the mixer," Diane planned as she paged through that section in her book. "There is still some bread in the freezer that we can use, and I can use one of my frozen pie shells to make a pie. I can't peel potatoes though . . ." Her voice trailed off.

"I'm at your service, ma'am," Peter promised. "I'll peel potatoes and wash dishes and do whatever you tell me to do."

"Thank you, Peter," Diane said, smiling. "I'm sure we'll get along all right now. You wanted a simple meal anyway; why don't we just make a casserole and a salad? That way, we won't need to wash as many dishes. We could open a jar of fruit instead of making a pudding to eat with the cake. Will that be all right with you?"

"Of course it will be, Diane. I'm so glad I won't need to tell them that they can't come. Now, what should I do first?"

As they worked together that afternoon, Diane marveled at how quickly her tasks disappeared. Long before suppertime, she told Peter that nothing more needed to be done in the kitchen.

"Fine," he said. "Now we'll have time to study for Sunday school tomorrow and to relax awhile before bedtime."

The next afternoon, Peter and Diane watched from the living room window as their visitors drove away. Seeing Diane wave happily, Peter turned to her and asked, "How was your visit with Carol today? From the look on your face, you must have enjoyed it."

"I did, immensely," Diane returned, her face shining. "Carol and I have so many things in common, and it was easy to visit with her. She even thanked me for not preparing an elaborate meal, and then she washed all the dishes for me. And the twins played nicely by themselves. Did you notice that they picked up most of the toys and put them away?"

"So, was it worth the trouble we went through to show hospitality to them?" Peter asked. His eyes twinkled as he emphasized the word *hospitality*.

"It certainly was," Diane assured him. She settled herself on the sofa and reached for the church papers. Before starting to read, she laid them down again.

"Why is it," she wondered aloud, "that so often we dread doing the things we know we should do? Then when we deal with our pride and do those things anyway, we find we've been depriving ourselves of a blessing."

Peter looked up from the concordance that he had opened at his desk. "Why, indeed?" he mused.

14

Janice and the Preacher

"Look, Janice." Becky nudged her friend as the two stood together after church one Sunday morning. Becky held a program in her hand. "Did you see that Brother Harold Fisher will be speaking at the all-day Bible conference at Crescent Peak this week? Don't you remember how we appreciated his classes at Bible school last winter?"

"Of course I remember," Janice responded eagerly, her dark eyes sparkling.

"I expect," Becky went on, "that his messages must be every bit as interesting as his classes are. I want to be sure to attend those meetings, especially since he will be speaking."

"Same here," Janice agreed. "Why, just one of

his messages would make that two-hour trip worthwhile!"

"Oh, come on," Becky laughed. "You're not going to *worship* Brother Harold, are you?"

Janice chuckled. "Of course not. But do you remember that we had agreed that Brother Harold Fisher was our favorite teacher?"

"Yes, but I liked several others almost as well," Becky said. "I see that my parents want to go home now. I'll look forward to seeing you again this evening."

During the following week, Janice often thought about the coming meetings. The more she thought about them, the more she looked forward to hearing Brother Harold's messages. She had always appreciated his open, straightforward manner and his commonsense approach to issues. *Perhaps,* she thought, *he will still remember me and maybe even talk to me. After all, wasn't I in two of his classes at Bible school?*

Janice obtained a copy of the program and pinned it beside the mirror on her bedroom wall. After several days, she had memorized all of it. As she looked over it, it seemed to her that the titles of Brother Harold's messages sounded the most interesting.

Once, while she and her sister folded the laundry, Janice remembered Becky's laughing question

Sunday morning. *Of course I wouldn't do anything so silly as worship Brother Harold,* Janice told herself firmly. *I'm almost nineteen years old. Only children do things like that. I only appreciate him for what he is.* But somehow, that declaration did not comfort her as she had expected it to.

Friday morning dawned clear and bright. "I'm sure," Janice told her younger sister, "that after all the rain this week, it will be sunny for the meetings today."

"Don't get excited," Carol warned her. "It rains easily these days, you know."

"Rain or no rain, we have to get to church on time," Janice returned as she skipped downstairs.

A little later, the girls had finished setting the table and preparing breakfast. *What takes them so long to finish the chores this morning?* Janice wondered impatiently. She paced from one side of the kitchen to the other. Her hands rearranged the plants on the windowsill as she watched for the sight of her brothers and father coming for breakfast. To herself, she murmured, *It would be too bad if I had to miss hearing Brother Harold's interesting message this morning.*

Just then, her ten-year-old brother ran into the house. "Father says to wait a bit with breakfast," he panted. "Daisy freshened this morning, and her calf has some trouble. It might be fifteen minutes yet until they can come."

"Why not sooner?" Janice snapped at him. "Don't they know we have to hurry this morning? We have to drive two hours to get to Crescent Peak."

Robert looked at Janice, puzzled. "I'm sure they know that," he said finally and went back to the barn.

Mother appeared from the bedroom, carrying baby Louise. "Now, Janice, please don't lose your patience," she said. "We all want to get to church on time, and I'm sure the boys are hurrying. Why don't you sit and darn a few of these socks while you wait?"

A short time later, Janice heard the boys stamping their boots on the porch and went to meet them. "Leave your boots outside," she told them. "I don't have time to sweep up after you this morning."

"I know we're later than we should be," Kenneth said. "But if we hadn't helped that calf right away, it would likely not have lived until evening. Daisy has a nice-looking heifer calf. You should come out and see it sometime."

Janice glared at him. "I can't right now. And don't stand there just talking. We'll never get to church at this rate."

Kenneth chuckled. "Calm down, calm down,

sister. I'll help you with the dishes, if that helps you any."

When everyone finally settled into the van, Janice sighed with relief. *Maybe we'll still get there in time for Brother Harold's message,* she thought. *I can hardly wait!*

The rain-soaked trees beside the road dripped crystal drops in the morning sunshine. As Janice watched the trees whizzing past, a faint sense of foreboding came over her. She scanned the creek as they passed it and was dismayed to notice that it had nearly overflowed its banks. Knowing they would soon reach the river, she craned her neck to watch the road in front.

They rounded another bend, and Father quickly brought the van to a stop. Janice gasped in dismay to see that water covered the road. There, where a bridge used to stand, she could see only a swirling, muddy torrent. A barrier spanned the road, and a sign proclaimed what she had already guessed: "Bridge Out."

"Well," Father said, "that means we'll need to go all the way to Hinkley to get across the river. Going through Belmont might be closer, but that bridge is lower than this one. It will surely have water flowing over it, if it is still standing."

Janice groaned. Rapid calculations told her that even with no more delays, they would arrive at

Crescent Peak nearly an hour after the meeting started.

Robert was amused at this turn of events. "Let's sing," he begged. "We'll have time to sing lots of songs now."

Janice shot him a warning glance.

" 'Come, we that love the Lord,' " he started heartily. " 'And let our joys be known . . .' "

"I don't have many joys," Janice grumbled darkly. "We're going to be late for those special all-day meetings!"

Robert leaned toward Carol. "Better not talk to Janice," he whispered loudly. "She might blow up!"

Mother caught Robert's eye. "Don't exaggerate, Robert," she said sternly. "That wasn't very kind either."

Robert hung his head for a moment. "Sorry," he said. "I didn't really mean it."

Mother smiled at him, and then she smiled encouragingly at Janice. "I know you are disappointed," she said softly. "But let's try to make the best of this situation, since we can't change it."

Janice turned her face toward the window and bit her lip. *How could anyone be so cheerful right now?* The songs of the family swirled around her, but she did not join them. The scenery beyond the window drifted past, unseen. Tears welled up in her eyes, and she blinked them back. *Why does it seem as if everything needed to go wrong today, of all days?*

As the minutes ticked by, she slowly resigned herself to what she was sure would be the biggest disappointment she had ever faced. By the time Janice and her family arrived at Crescent Peak, she had decided to put on a cheerful face. After all, it would not do to let her friends see her disappointment.

As they entered the building, Janice felt relieved. "Good," she whispered to Carol. "They are singing the song between the messages. So we are still in time to hear Brother Harold."

As she settled into her chair, Janice scanned the speakers on the platform. *Why isn't Brother Harold among them? Perhaps he will come later,* she consoled herself. She reached for a songbook and joined in the singing.

When the song was over, Brother Harold still had not appeared. Janice looked around expectantly, hoping to catch a glimpse of him bustling up the aisle.

But wait. What was the moderator saying? "Because of the absence of Brother Harold Fisher, we will look to Brother David Adams for the second message of the morning."

Janice gasped. Her uncle would be taking Brother Harold's place! She had often heard him preach. Now she would have to listen to him again instead of Brother Harold, whom she had looked forward to hearing for so long. She sat up a bit straighter and struggled to keep her composure.

Her uncle's calm voice broke into her tumbling thoughts. "Brother Harold notified us this morning that sickness in his family makes it impossible for him to be here. The committee asked me to take his place this morning."

His next words startled Janice. "Those of you who came to hear Brother Harold Fisher will be disappointed. The rest of us will look to the Lord and receive a blessing from Him."

Janice bowed her head, ashamed. *Of course,* she told herself. *How could I have lost sight of the real reason for having Bible conference?* She thought again of Becky's question: "You're not going to worship Brother Harold, are you?" Now, however, the question did not seem funny. Soberly, Janice realized that she had anticipated Brother Harold's words more than she had looked for a message from God. She remembered how impatient she had been at the prospect of missing Brother Harold, and she bowed her head still farther.

"Father," she prayed silently, "I've failed again. I've been guilty of the very thing I said I wouldn't do, and have allowed my carnal desires to overrule my hunger for Your message to me. I'm sorry, and I'm also sorry for my impatience this morning. Please help me to make that right with my family. And may I glean from Uncle David's message the truths You want me to learn."

Reaching for a tissue, Janice wiped several tears from her face. Lifting her head determinedly, she sat up to give her full attention to the remainder of the service.

15

"What Picture?"

Linda hummed to herself as she guided her sweeper under her brother's bed and around the dresser. *I'm almost done cleaning Roger's room,* she told herself. *Then I have only my own to do, and I'll be finished up here for today. It surely is nice to get the upstairs cleaning done on Thursday for a change.*

A sweet, smiling face on the dresser caught her attention. *Hmm. I see that Beth must have given a picture of herself to Roger recently.* Linda gazed at her brother's girlfriend for several moments. Then a thought popped into her head. *Roger knows how Beth looks by now,* she decided. *He's been seeing her for a whole year already. I'll just turn the picture around and see what he says about it.* With one swift motion, she pulled the picture from the frame and inserted it backward so that only the white backing showed through the glass. *There now, won't he be surprised?* she congratulated herself. Then she turned and picked up her sweeper and dustcloth, ready to leave the room.

A small movement at the door made Linda stop and stare. Her four-year-old sister, Ruthanne, stood there, calmly surveying her older sister. "Mother says you can come downstairs and start dinner now," Ruthanne announced when she saw Linda eyeing her. "We would like to eat dinner earlier today, since Father and the boys want to help Uncle Luke this afternoon."

"All right," Linda consented. "Let me put my things away first." She stepped across the hall to deposit her sweeper in the closet, and Ruthanne started down the stairs. *How long was she standing there watching me?* Linda wondered. *Oh, well, she knows by now that we like to have our fun sometimes.* Linda closed the door and followed her sister down the steps.

While Linda washed the dishes after dinner, Ruthanne dried them, and their brothers disappeared upstairs to change into clean clothes. Linda listened to their footsteps overhead as she swished the dishes through her water. Sure enough, one

set of footsteps turned around and came downstairs again.

"Where is my picture?" Roger demanded. "Did
you do something with the picture on my dresser,
Linda?"

Linda turned to face him and tried to look as
candid as possible. "What picture?" she asked,
pulling a bowl out of the rinse water.

"Why, the picture of Beth, of course," Roger
answered. "You know something about it, don't
you?"

Linda dropped her eyes to hide her amusement.
"I didn't see any picture on your dresser when I
finished cleaning this morning," she told him.
"Maybe you'd better look a little harder. I'm sure
it has to be somewhere around."

Roger looked at her for a long moment. Then
he turned and went upstairs again, and Linda
returned to her dishes.

That evening after supper, Roger confronted
her just outside his room. "I still haven't found
it," he told her. "And I'm sure you did something
with that picture."

Linda grinned at him. "Then you haven't looked
hard enough," she answered. "It can't be very far
from where it used to be." She ducked into her
room before he could ask her any more questions.

The next morning, Linda had nearly forgotten

about Roger's problem. Since he did not mention anything about it, she assumed that he had found his picture. *Serves him right though,* she declared to the eggs as she fried them. *If I couldn't have any fun around here, I'd . . .* She was not sure what she would do, but her father and brothers came in for breakfast just then, so Linda left the deciding until later.

After breakfast, Linda hurried to get a casserole into the oven for her brothers to eat at dinnertime, since neither she nor Mother would be at home for most of the day. As she peeled potatoes, Mother finished washing the rest of the dishes.

"Come, Ruthanne," Mother called next. "I want to comb your hair now; then you'll be ready to go along to the sewing."

Ruthanne came running from the living room, pulling at her pigtails. "I can undo my braids by myself already," she declared. "See, here are my rubber bands."

Mother smiled and reached for the hairbrush. "You're growing up," she agreed. "Oh, I forgot to bring some water." Mother hurried over to the sink for a small dish into which to dip her hairbrush. When she returned, Ruthanne had already undone her hair and sat waiting, an expectant sparkle in her eyes.

Linda held up the bowl full of potatoes she had

peeled. "Will this be enough for dinner?" she asked. "I want to make sure they don't run short."

Mother looked up, her fingers still flying. "Peel about three more. Here, Ruthanne; where did you put your rubber bands?"

Ruthanne tipped up her head and looked innocent. "What rubber bands?" she asked.

"The rubber bands that you took out of your hair," Mother replied, astonished. "You just took them out a minute ago. Where did you put them?"

Ruthanne looked around, as if surprised by the question. "I don't see any rubber bands around here, do you?" she replied.

Mother put her hand under Ruthanne's chin and pulled her face upward. Then she looked full into the child's face. "Now, Ruthanne," she began, "you know where you put those rubber bands. I will need to punish you for lying to me. But first, get me those rubber bands so that I can finish your hair."

Ruthanne got up and picked up two rubber bands from the chair where she had been sitting. "But Linda does that," she declared as she handed them to Mother and sat down again.

"Linda does?" Mother sounded shocked. "When does Linda hide rubber bands?" Her eyes sought Linda's, but Linda suddenly found something very interesting on the potato she was peeling and did not look up.

"Linda hides things and forgets where she puts them," Ruthanne insisted. "Anyway, she did yesterday when she hid Roger's picture. And last night I was playing with my dolly on the steps, and she did it again."

Mother paused. "What Linda did makes no difference to you," she explained firmly. "When you hid your rubber bands and pretended not to know where they were, you were acting a lie. Lying is not allowed in this house. I will have to punish you for lying to me, as I said. After this, you will not do such a thing again. Do you understand?"

Ruthanne nodded tearfully. In a minute, Mother snapped the rubber band on her second braid. "Now come with me to the bedroom," she said, taking Ruthanne's hand. Linda watched them go, and the look Ruthanne threw her seemed to cut her to the heart.

A short time later, Mother reentered the kitchen. She picked up a paring knife and started to slice potatoes into the roaster with astounding speed. After what felt like an hour to Linda, Mother spoke, and her voice was low and soft. "Do you know anything about Roger's picture? What did Ruthanne mean by what she said?"

"Oh, that was yesterday," Linda said, and the words seemed to push each other out of her mouth. "When I was cleaning upstairs, I just turned his picture of Beth around in the frame. I didn't really hide it, and anyway, I just wanted to tease him a bit. I didn't realize Ruthanne was watching me when I did it."

Mother sighed, and her knife slowed just a little. "How often must I tell you that the younger ones will do anything you older ones do? I'm disappointed in the example you've been to Ruthanne in this situation."

"But I was only teasing," Linda objected.

"Only teasing?" Mother asked. "Do you think Roger thought so? And were you being kind to him?"

Linda hung her head and felt the tears pushing at her eyes. "I know he didn't appreciate it," she had to admit. "But I thought he should be able to take a bit of teasing."

"And was he able?" Mother wondered.

"I—I guess he did get a little upset at it," Linda admitted.

"Linda, Linda," Mother said sadly. "You know that we don't want you to tease your brother about his girlfriend. Courtship is much too serious to take it lightly. Besides, I told Ruthanne she was acting a lie when she pretended she did not know where she put her rubber bands. Weren't you doing the same thing to Roger?"

Linda paused. "I suppose. I guess I should apologize."

"Yes," Mother answered kindly, "you should. You might want to explain to Ruthanne as well, since she took an example from what you did."

Mother picked up the last white potato and finished slicing it. "Now, understand," she explained, "we don't mind when our children enjoy life. However, you must remember the Golden Rule, even in your teasing. As long as one person needs to feel bad about what you are doing, then you are not being kind. You can have enjoyment and yet be kind to each other. Don't you think so?"

Linda nodded slowly. "I might have to look for those ways until I get used to thinking about them," she said, "but I'm sure I can find them. Do I have time to find Roger before we leave?"

"Yes, of course," Mother answered. "I'll finish this casserole. And after this, I'll be ready to help you in any other way as well."

"Thank you, Mother," Linda replied. "I appreciate that."

16

Letters and Promises

Susan sighed as she slit another envelope. *So much mail every day.* Although she enjoyed her job as secretary for her uncle's welding shop, the never-ending cycle of bookkeeping and filing sometimes loomed large. It was Tuesday already, and it seemed she had not accomplished anything yet that week.

Large letters at the top of the paper in her hand caught her attention: DO NOT THROW THIS LETTER AWAY! Susan took a second look. Then, curious, she scanned the rest of the sheet. Her eyes narrowed over what she saw. "This is not a chain letter. This letter was sent to bring you good luck," it said. "You must make twenty copies of this letter and pass them on within ninety-six hours, or else you will forfeit your good luck and invite bad luck." The letter then went on to give several accounts of people who had lost their homes or their jobs within days of ignoring this particular letter. Apparently, one man had even lost his wife. "The original is in New England," it stated next. "This good-luck letter has been going on for fifteen years, and it has been around the world nine times. Please don't break the circuit."

Susan turned the sheet over, looking for a clue as to who had sent it. Nothing. The envelope had no return address, and the postmark was blurred. She read the letter again. Could it be true? She laid it on her desk and turned to the rest of the mail. As her fingers flew, her mind mulled over what she had just read. What if it were true? Should she—but no, Uncle Allen would likely not believe it. He would probably not appreciate her using postage and envelopes for such a cause without telling him about it. What should she do then? Should she use her own envelopes and postage? Susan could not decide which would be better. So she laid the paper in her drawer and went on with her work. *After all, I have four days to decide,* she told herself. *By that time I will surely have figured out something.*

But the sheet of paper in her drawer would not

stay there. During the rest of the day, Susan wondered many times about what would happen further. It even seemed as if she had more than the usual number of interruptions. By the end of the day, she was glad to lock the door and go home.

Even there, the letter haunted her. It bothered her thoughts and seemed to follow her about the house. When her brother came in from the barn nursing a bleeding hand, she had all she could do to stifle a scream. Were the bad things happening already, just because she could not decide what to do about that letter? If they were, then she would make those copies and send them away first thing in the morning. It would be no problem to pick twenty names from her list of customers.

With that decided, Susan felt a little better. Somehow, she finished the rest of that evening. She kept a careful watch for anything out of the ordinary. No need to invite disaster. But try as she might, she could not find peace in her heart about the decision she had made. An uneasy fear kept her from her usual happiness, and she kept wondering what would happen next.

In the morning, Susan looked at the letter for a long time. Then she put it back into her drawer. *I just can't bring myself to do it,* she decided. *Maybe by tomorrow, something will turn up and I'll know for sure what to do.*

On Friday morning, Susan paused just before she entered her office. *Oh, yes,* she remembered, *today I will have to tell Uncle Allen about that letter. I wonder what he will say about it.*

Just then, Uncle Allen met her at the door. "Don't bother turning on your computer," he said. "It wouldn't run if you wanted it to."

Susan stopped, and at the same moment she noticed that everything was dark and quiet. "What's wrong?" she gasped. "That rack order is only half done, and we can't stop the welders yet."

"No, we can hardly stop the welders yet," Uncle Allen agreed. "But we have to anyhow. We don't have electricity here this morning, and they tell me the night shift worked only half a shift. I'm just on my way to see if I can find something in the electrical room."

Susan turned and followed him to the small room behind the offices. It did not take long for Uncle Allen to fish a flashlight out of his pocket and shine it onto the wall where all the large relays and switches hung. He let out a long whistle, and Susan looked over his shoulder to see what he saw. The sight made her stomach lurch. One whole box was charred and black, with a ragged hole blown into the cover. The plywood wall behind the row of switch boxes was black and smoky.

By this time, several curious faces darkened the

doorway. "See that, boys?" Uncle Allen asked, motioning toward the wall. He opened the box and revealed more ragged edges where two of the heavy wires had melted off their sockets. "That was a big bang," he remarked. "I don't see what kept it from burning the wall and the rest of the building."

"God did." This came from Susan's cousin David.

"Yes, of course," Uncle Allen agreed. "And I'm thankful for His protection. Does anyone know when this might have happened?"

Shaken, Susan quietly returned to her office under cover of the general discussion that followed. *How can they be so calm?* she asked herself. *All of them know that we nearly lost this building during the night sometime—and all the equipment.* She shuddered at the thought. Just last year, another shop in the area had burned down, and the owner had needed to go out of business because of the loss he had sustained. *What if that had happened to us? Would it have been because of that letter in my drawer?*

Before very long, Uncle Allen came in and reached for the telephone. He arranged for an electrician to fix the problem in the switch box, and then he settled down to do some paperwork at his desk.

Here's my chance, Susan thought. Outwardly

calm, but inwardly trembling, she pulled the letter from her drawer and laid it on his desk. "What do you think of that?" she asked. Then she said no more for fear that her voice would betray her anxiety.

Uncle Allen read the letter without a comment. Then he looked up, chuckled, and reached for his calculator. For several minutes, he punched numbers and scribbled them onto a piece of scrap paper. Finally, he leaned toward Susan.

"Look here," he said, barely able to keep the chuckles out of his voice. "This letter makes some absurd claims. First, it is in fact a chain letter. And if it has been around for fifteen years, why did we never see it before?" He waved his piece of paper toward her. "According to these numbers, if the chain were never broken, the entire population of Canada would receive two letters in the first six weeks. In one week after that, everyone in the United States would receive four of these letters. Within the next two weeks, the whole population of the world would receive at least one letter. That's on top of the two that we Canadians received and the four that the Americans received. Can you imagine the blizzard of mail that would provoke?"

Susan had to grin just a bit in spite of herself. "But what about those stories of what happened to the people who ignored this letter?" she asked.

Uncle Allen cleared his throat. "Since it makes such ridiculous claims about how old it is, I don't believe the rest of it either, about all the bad luck these people supposedly had. We know that God has our lives in His control, and such a thing as making twenty copies of a fantastic letter won't necessarily bring God's blessing upon us."

Susan thought about that for a bit. Stated like that, the letter did sound a bit incredible.

Taking her silence for agreement, Uncle Allen crumpled the letter in his hand and dropped it into the wastebasket. "If you ask me," he said, "the world has no need of such letters. I am going to break the chain of this one."

Susan choked back a gasp at his matter-of-fact tone. "But aren't you afraid of what might happen?" she asked.

"Of course not," Uncle Allen replied. "In this situation, I am claiming God's promise that 'God hath not given us the spirit of fear; but of power, . . . and of a sound mind' and also 'He shall give his angels charge over thee, to keep thee in all thy ways.' We don't even know who sent it to us; for all we know, it was just a joke. Besides, we've just seen a beautiful example of God's protection—otherwise we wouldn't have any shop this morning." He turned back to his desk, and Susan had to be satisfied with that.

Several weeks later, Susan finished making up her monthly reports. As she looked them over, she marveled at how much business they had done recently. *It's almost as if God is especially blessing us,* she remarked to herself. Suddenly she remembered the chain letter that her uncle had thrown away. She smiled. *The bad luck we were supposed to have never came,* she decided. *And I'm glad for the lesson I learned about trusting God instead of putting trust in foolish promises. I hope I can always remember that.*

17

The Right Place at the Right Time

Daniel slid cautiously into the driver's seat as his sister slid into the passenger seat. *I haven't driven this diesel car very often,* he mused. He watched his father disappear through the swinging doors of the office of the construction company. *Let's see, Susan and I should have plenty of time to do this business before eleven-thirty. He told us we should be back by then.*

The car jerked as he slid it into gear. "Not very manly," Daniel remarked aloud. As he steered the car onto the highway, he thought about the location of the business he needed to find in the city.

I wish I had checked the location on a map. I don't want to become lost on those busy streets. And I don't relish driving this standard shift that much.

Since recently acquiring his license, Daniel had run errands around home for his father in their family business. This time, his father wanted Susan, his younger sister, and him to take a check to a business with which he was not well acquainted. "You can find it," Father had said. "You know the city fairly well. If you can't find it, just ask someone for directions. The business is large enough that it should be well known."

An hour later, as they entered the city limits, he again glanced at the address on the invoice that he had with him. "Hmm, Saskatchewan Street. That should be close to Manitoba Street. That means I should take this exit and go south three blocks before turning left again."

But after twenty minutes of fruitless searching, they still had not found the place they were looking for. Seeing a uniformed traffic attendant, Daniel stopped and rolled down his window. "Do you know where to find the company called Shelby Supply?"

The young man scratched his head. "No, I guess I don't. I'm new here, you see, and haven't been all over town yet. But I like your white cap," he said to Susan. "Why do you wear it?"

Daniel was startled by the sudden question, but

he managed to reply thoughtfully, "She wears it in obedience to the Bible. We love the Lord Jesus and want to obey whatever He asks of us. Do you know who Jesus is?"

The young man shifted uncomfortably. "Yes—I mean—I've heard of Him already." A gleam came into his eye, and he continued, "But I don't want anyone to preach to me about such sissy stuff."

Daniel reached over into the glove compartment and pulled out several tracts. "Here, take these. This one explains who we are, and this one tells more about the covering. And if you have any more questions, feel free to call the telephone number on the back."

The young man put the papers into his pocket and glanced down the street. "You'd better get going, or you'll be blocking the traffic."

As he waited at the next set of traffic lights, Daniel glanced into the rear-view mirror. The young man had seated himself on the curb and was engrossed in reading the small paper in his hand. "Please, Lord, let the seed that was sown bear fruit," he breathed.

After searching another street unsuccessfully, Daniel stopped his car again. "Lord," he prayed, "somehow I just can't find this place. Please show me the way to go."

"Maybe you can find some help there," Susan

said, indicating a small gas station nearby. Accordingly, Daniel stopped again.

"Do you have a city map here?" he asked the cashier.

"Sure, over there on the wall."

Daniel and Susan walked over to the map and studied it carefully. "Aha," said Daniel. "Saskatchewan Street *crosses* Manitoba, instead of running parallel with it, as I had thought. So I should go back to Clarke Avenue and head west again." A minute later, feeling satisfied that he had now planned his route well, they started out again.

"Now, the street I want should be right around here somewhere," he decided. He drove past two more street crossings and did not find it. Recognizing the next street name, he gasped in dismay. "I've driven too far again! I wonder, if I go over one block and head back, maybe I will find it that way."

Finally, after circling a small area three times, Daniel became frustrated. "Please, Lord," he prayed again, "I can't find this place by myself. I'll just go down this little side street once more. Saskatchewan Street *has* to be close by, surely!"

Sure enough, there it was. However, elation turned to discouragement as Daniel circled the large building belonging to Shelby Supply. "It doesn't do me any good to find the place if I can't park when I get there," he told Susan a bit impatiently.

After the second round, he slipped into a just-vacated parking spot. "Thank You, Lord," he breathed. "And thank You too for helping me with all this city driving."

Daniel scanned the building before him. "Now, where is the door to the offices?" he wondered. "I guess we'll just have to walk until we find it."

After entering at the big glass doors, they scanned the directory on the wall. "The office I want is on third floor," he said. "And this old building doesn't have elevators. Here goes!" He grinned. "If we want to get there, we'll have to take the stairs, I guess."

At the top of the second flight of steps, they paused for breath. "Good! Mr. Smith's office is right here, not far down the hall."

Daniel glanced at a woman sitting on a bench. The woman returned his glance. Curiously, she looked at Daniel and Susan more closely. Daniel stepped to the window and pulled out the check that his father had prepared.

The receptionist looked at the check. "Oh, I'm sorry, but I can't take this. No one signed it."

"Oh, no. How could we have overlooked that?" Daniel tried to quell his rising impatience. "Is there no way you can take it anyway?"

"Do you have signing rights on this account?"

"No, it's my father's account."

"Then I'm sorry, but we absolutely cannot take it this way. I see by your address that you came from a distance. But our bank simply won't take an unsigned check, and there is nothing I can do about that."

Silently, Daniel slipped the check into his bill-fold and started down the steps after Susan.

"Excuse me."

Daniel looked up. "Yes, how may I help you?" he asked. The woman who had been sitting on the bench outside Mr. Smith's office came up to them.

"Ah, please, I was just wondering. How come you didn't get upset there at the office?" Pointing at Susan's covering, she added, "Does it have anything to do with her white cap? I notice you both dress differently from most people. Does that have anything to do with it? Most people I know would have at least yelled, and maybe even cursed, if they had something like that happen to them. How did you stay so calm?"

So, for the second time that morning, Daniel testified of his love for his Lord. Later, as he shifted the car into gear and joined the stream of traffic, he pondered his experiences. "Maybe it wasn't such a wild-goose chase after all," he concluded. "Who knows? Probably God intended to bring those two souls into contact with the Gospel and put us in the right place at the right time to accomplish it."

" 'Choose my path, O blessed Saviour,' " Susan sang out. Daniel joined in heartily. " 'Order Thou my steps, dear Saviour, / Just as seemeth good to Thee.' "

18

Of Lessons in Stories

Doris let her eyes travel all the way around the quilt. "You'd think we mothers hardly ever saw each other," she remarked to Janet, seated around the corner. "At least judging by the way we talk on sewing circle days."

Janet smiled as she stitched. "It certainly seems like we have a lot to catch up on," she agreed.

Doris took another stitch; then she leaned closer to Janet. "Is it true," she wondered, lowering her voice, "that Chad and Margaret are having problems in their marriage? I heard that he can hardly hold a job and that she doesn't like that."

"No wife would," Janet replied quietly. "But remember, they've been Christians for only about a year now, and before that they lived in the city. He's working for my husband's framing crew now, and I believe he really wants to do what's right. But I don't want to sit here and gossip about them." Her eyes twinkled as she looked up from her needlework. "Why don't you write a story instead? One that would help them see how to get along."

"Oh, but I can't," Doris protested.

"Why not?" Janet returned. "You and John seem to get along quite well. Surely you have some ideas on the subject."

"But that's different," Doris returned. "I can't just preach about our marriage. No one likes a sermon like that."

Janet nodded. "I know it's hard to give someone the answers when they haven't asked the questions," she agreed. "But most people will appreciate the lesson in an interesting story. Besides, it's not as though you've never written before."

Doris blushed and pushed her needle in and out, in and out, in and out of the quilt. "Yes, write," the Spirit spoke clearly to her. "Remember My promise, 'I will guide thee.' "

Immediately an incident popped into her mind that would make a plot for a story on relationships. As Doris pondered it, she looked up to meet

Janet's still-twinkling eyes. "Maybe I could give it a try," she consented.

"Not just 'maybe,' " Janet urged. "I'll be looking for that story—and right soon."

"Say, Doris," someone asked just then, "are you nearly finished quilting there in the corner? We'll soon be waiting on you two."

"Almost," Doris replied, and the conversation about writing ended.

That afternoon, as the ladies gathered their coats and purses together, Janet made her way to Doris. "Now don't forget," she said, her eyes twinkling. "I'll be looking for that story from you."

Doris smiled. "Oh, you!"

"Make it soon," Janet added as she went out the door.

As Doris drove home that afternoon, she could not shake the feeling that she must write this story soon. *How many people need help with their marriage relationships?* she pondered. As she kept on thinking, the couple in her story grew to almost-real proportions.

Over the next several days, Doris pondered her story. Finally, she had it all planned out. *Now, for time to write it down,* she thought. *I know this is an important subject.*

Time went on. One day followed another, and the story did not get written.

One day Doris realized with a start that nearly three months had passed since she had agreed to write that story. *Three months lost,* she admitted to herself. *Today I really must start it.* Then the baby cried, John needed a button sewed on his coat, and one thing followed another until suddenly it was time to prepare supper for her family. So another day passed by.

As time went on, Doris nearly forgot about the story she had planned to write. Yet sometimes, in the strangest places, it would intrude on her thoughts. It seemed as if the couple in her story begged her, "You must tell our story. It's important!" And Doris would answer, "Yes, yes, I know. But there are so many other important things to do." Every time she met Margaret or Chad, a stab would go through her heart and she would feel sorry for them again. They did try so hard, after all.

Then, one Sunday morning after the church service, Doris met Margaret in tears in the mothers' room. "I don't know what to do anymore," Margaret lamented. "I've tried so hard to make a happy home for our family. It seems nothing works anymore."

Doris felt tears start down her own cheeks. "God still loves you," she told Margaret. "He'll give you grace for whatever you need to do. I'd like to help you too, if I could."

"I know you would," Margaret agreed. She sat in the rocking chair, staring at her fingers. "But you and John get along so well, I can't imagine you ever having struggles like ours."

"Oh, but we don't always agree either," Doris replied. "But we try to resolve our differences without getting angry at each other."

Margaret lifted her eyes and looked at Doris for just a moment. "I know I get too angry at Chad," she mumbled. "I can't seem to help it." She heaved a deep sigh. "I guess I never learned how to control myself, as you did. You know, my mother always acted like this."

"I can understand," Doris told her. Then both women were silent while Doris prayed quietly for more wisdom.

The door opened, and Margaret's two little girls came into the room. "Oh, here you are, Mother," exclaimed the older one. "Father said he's ready to go now. Look, we got some more story papers to read. Isn't that nice, Mother?"

Margaret looked down at the little girl and took the church papers from her hand. She sucked in her breath and held out the *Christian Example* for Doris to read the title on the front page. " 'A Happy Marriage,' " Doris read. A glance over the paper showed that this was indeed a story, not an article.

Margaret gave Doris a thin smile and got up to

follow her two girls out the door. "Thanks for listening," she said. "And thanks for your encouragement. I'll read this story, and maybe I'll talk to you again at the service this evening. Have a good afternoon."

Feeling stunned, Doris picked up her own baby and then followed her husband to their car. When she opened their own church papers, she felt more stunned than ever as she read the story that started on the front of the *Christian Example*. It followed very nearly the same outline she had been contemplating in her own heart.

"Why so quiet?" John asked as they washed the dishes together after lunch. "Thinking?"

"Yes, thinking," she agreed, "and feeling chastened."

"Oh?" he wondered. "How is that?"

Doris wiped her hands and went to fetch the church papers. "Here; look at this," she told him. "That's almost exactly the same story I was planning to write—and never did." She recounted her conversation with Margaret and how cheered she had appeared at the prospect of reading a story about the blessings of someone else's marriage. "I feel that the Lord knew someone would need that story; and since I didn't write it, He had to get someone else to write it. This makes me wonder if every story I'm inspired to write will meet someone's specific need after it's printed."

John looked thoughtful. "I wouldn't be surprised," he said finally. "After all, God knows the needs of each person. He's certainly interested in meeting those needs. And most certainly our enemy would like to stop that process."

"I've never been chastened quite like this before," Doris admitted. "But after this, I want to be more faithful in writing the things God inspires me with."

"God will bless you for that, I'm sure," John answered. "Your duties as a mother and wife do come first, but that should not keep you from writing that occasional, needed story that the Lord wants from you."

19

One Moment's Decision

That day last summer turned out to be the warmest day of the whole year. But I didn't know that when I promised Mrs. Forbes that I would deliver her straw. Elderly Mrs. Forbes lives by herself and raises horses. Because of her severe arthritis, her son and daughter-in-law help her most of the time. And since her husband died, she relies on me and my boys to provide her with hay and straw. Usually we have no problem with the arrangement. But then, she had never run out of straw in July before.

By the time I arrived at her barns with my tractor and the two wagonloads of bales, I already regretted the fact that I had forgotten my jug of water. So I was unusually glad when her son Max met me and offered to help unload the bales. "And when we're finished," he said, "Mom will pay you, and my wife will bring us something cold to drink."

"Thank you very much," I told him, with one eye on the sun. "I'm sure we'll appreciate it by then."

Unloading went well, except that we had to stop more often to rest. A man can work only so fast when he's as hot as we were and dripping with sweat. Max proved to be a good helper; so in good time we had finished.

"Now for our drinks," Max rejoiced, leading the way to the picnic table under the shade tree.

Mrs. Forbes saw us coming and called out through the kitchen window, "We'll be right there."

I must admit that I have seldom looked forward to a glass of cold water as much as I did right then. So imagine my surprise when Mrs. Forbes came hobbling around the corner of the house, followed by her daughter-in-law, who was clutching four big brown beer bottles in her arms. I closed my eyes and groaned ever so softly. Instantly the tempter whispered to me, "Just a swallow can't hurt. Nobody ever got drunk on that little. Just drink a little so you won't offend the dear old lady. Then you can leave the rest. Nothing wrong with that, is there?"

But I shook my head and opened my eyes. The younger Mrs. Forbes set all four of the bottles in a row on the table, and then she looked at me. I saw her about ready to say "Help yourself," but instead she said, "Why, Mr. Martin! What is wrong?"

For an instant, I wavered. Then I said, "I'm sorry, Karina. I was looking for just water, since we don't drink alcohol."

She looked astonished. "We can't drink the water here," she said. "Our water is bad unless we boil it. Can I bring you a soda instead?"

"Oh, I'll be all right," I said. "Really. Please don't bother." The fizz bubbling out of those bottles made me thirstier than ever. But I knew I would be going home in a few minutes, just as soon as they paid me for the straw. Surely I could survive until then.

Karina helped Mrs. Forbes settle herself painfully onto the bench. Then she headed for the house. "It's no problem," Karina assured me. "Let me do this for you."

In a very short time, she handed me a soda, and I immediately drank deeply of the cold liquid.

Old Mrs. Forbes waited until I stopped for a breath, and then she blurted out her question: "How come you folks don't drink? Is it because your church says you can't?"

I had to finish swallowing before I could answer. "Well, yes," I said. "Our church requires us to avoid all kinds of strong drink. But I would anyway because of what the Bible says about it."

Quick as a cough, she asked, "The Bible?" Then she repeated it and added, "Does the Bible say anything about beer?"

I pulled my small Bible from my pocket and read to them the verses in Proverbs 23: " 'Who hath woe? who hath sorrow? who hath contentions? who hath babbling? who hath wounds without cause? who hath redness of eyes? They that tarry long at the wine; they that go to seek mixed wine. Look not thou upon the wine when it is red, when it giveth his colour in the cup, when it moveth itself aright. At the last it biteth like a serpent, and stingeth like an adder.' " When I looked up again, all three of them were listening with all their might. Karina had tears in her eyes, and Max was nodding his head slowly.

"All of that is true, and much more," Max said.

"There's more," I told them. "Like this one: 'Wine is a mocker, strong drink is raging: and whosoever is deceived thereby is not wise.' "

Max kept on nodding his head, so after a bit I went on. "And here's another one: 'Woe unto them that rise up early in the morning, that they may follow strong drink; that continue until night, till wine inflame them . . . [and] they regard not the work of the LORD, neither consider the operation of his hands. Therefore my people are gone into captivity, because they have no knowledge: and their honourable men are famished, and their multitude dried up with thirst.' "

"Powerful words, those," Max offered. "I know they speak the truth." He hung his head, and I had a feeling that he understood the words I had read better than I did.

I tried to explain to Max that he did not need to perish, that the love of God could cleanse even someone like him. He listened carefully, nodding the whole time.

Karina, Max's wife, silently listened to the whole conversation. When I finished, she looked into his eyes and said, "Well, then, what am I doing with this?" She took her bottle and pushed it as far across the table as she could reach. "I'm quitting right now," she said, smiling up at him.

Max looked at her for a long moment. Then he pushed his bottle across the table and set it beside hers. "I'm quitting too," he said. "Now we'll have to help each other with the withdrawal."

"Hey, you two!" Mrs. Forbes sputtered. "If you can, I can too." She pushed her bottle across the table too.

"Better yet," I suggested, "why don't you start

right now by dumping the beer out of these bottles so you won't be tempted to finish them?"

Without a word, Max stood up and grabbed all four bottles in his big hands. He tipped them over, and we watched as four streams disappeared into the grass under the table.

As I said, that was last summer. Now, whenever I meet Max or Karina, they always act happy to see me. I am trying to tell them that without Jesus they still have not found the true peace and joy that He alone can give. But I am thankful every time they tell me that they still stay away from strong drink and that they have never been drunk since that day.

Whatever comes of their story, I will be forever grateful that God's grace helped me to resist the temptation to join them in their drinking. Who knows? Perhaps the course of future generations was hanging on that decision of one moment.

20

Only Remembered

As she followed her brother and her parents into the large church auditorium, Kathy suppressed a gasp. Soft light from the stained-glass windows fell upon the bank of flowers at the front of the room. Several large heart-shaped wreaths nearly buried the casket below the pulpit. Huge bouquets of roses stood here and there among the plush pews.

The four Weavers joined the line that moved slowly past the casket. As Kathy stood in line, she could not help comparing this room with the simple, unadorned building in which she normally worshiped.

Mr. Matthew Henderson must have been quite

well-to-do, Kathy decided when she stood in front of the ornately carved wooden casket. The body inside lay dressed in an expensive silk-and-velvet suit. A diamond ring adorned one finger, and the cold, lifeless hands clutched a golden chain that clipped onto a large gold watch.

Kathy turned to shake hands with the sobbing widow and her daughter. Both of them looked utterly hopeless.

"He cherished that watch so much," the lady was saying between sobs. "His father gave it to him for his fortieth birthday, and he often told me how much it meant to him. When he knew he was dying, his last request was that it should be buried with him." A note of bitterness crept into the lady's cultured voice as she added, "He wanted people to see it and remember him as the man whose expensive gold watch was buried with him."

"Oh," Kathy said. To herself she thought, *What a vain thing to remember him by! I wonder what the rest of his life was like.* Just then her mother nudged her, and Kathy turned to follow the rest of her family to a pew.

Grand organ music swirled around them while the rest of the people were seated. As she waited for the service to begin, Kathy examined the colorful stained-glass window beside her. Near the top, a band of small blue blocks outlined a circle in which a delicate gray dove floated. Waves of delicate purple, light green, yellow, and orange cascaded halfway down the window, where they all came together in a breathtaking design. Below that, a row of pink roses, supported by a brown panel, marched across the width of the window. At the very bottom, a soft gray panel proclaimed: "Donated by Matthew Henderson."

"Matthew Henderson!" Kathy whispered to herself. *Why, his funeral is right now, and he will be buried yet today.* She caught Jonathan's eye and motioned toward the window, pointing out the name at the bottom. "See that?" she asked him quietly.

Jonathan's eyes widened when he read the panel. Kathy could see that the wheels of his mind were spinning, but he did not say anything. Just then a robed minister stepped behind the pulpit to begin the service.

After the short service, several men carried the casket outside and a hearse took it away. When no one made a move to follow, the Weavers joined the stream of people flowing downstairs to partake of the refreshments.

After Kathy received her plate of dainty cookies and a glass of juice, she glanced around for an empty place to sit. *Ah, over there is our landlady,* she decided. *I'm sure she goes to church here. I'll sit beside her.* So saying, she made her way down the row of chairs to where Mrs. Fraser sat.

"Good afternoon, Mrs. Fraser," Kathy greeted her neighbor. "Did you know Mr. Henderson well?"

"Sure did," Mrs. Fraser answered readily. "Why do you ask? Didn't you know him? You live beside the Hendersons, don't you?"

"Yes, we do," Kathy admitted. "But we've been living here only three months, you know, and he was sick most of that time. I'm wondering what kind of man he was before that. I noticed that he donated a window to this church. Aren't windows like that quite expensive?"

Mrs. Fraser nodded, and her painted face suddenly lost its pleasant look. "Matthew Henderson was always like that," she said, lowering her voice slightly. "He did things that people noticed, things that took much money. But the real Matthew Henderson was mean to his wife and ugly to his children. I suppose you know he broke his son's arm once. Matthew was angry with him for something or other, and he simply took the boy's arm into his hands and twisted it until it broke."

Kathy gasped. "I didn't know that. I didn't even know that he had a son. I thought Barbara was all the family they had."

"Oh, no," Mrs. Fraser answered, shaking her earrings. "They had two boys too. Both of them got tired of their mean father, so they ran away and joined the military. Mrs. Henderson and Barbara stuck it out only because they knew there would be a big inheritance for them when it was all over." Here she lowered her voice still further and leaned toward Kathy. "And there is! Mark my word, Kathy! Those two women will be well provided for, for the rest of their days. For all his meanness, Matthew Henderson was rich enough."

Kathy sat numbly, trying to comprehend what this talkative lady was telling her. "So do you mean," she ventured finally, "that Mr. Henderson left nothing to the two boys?"

"Absolutely nothing! He was upset at their running away, and he often said that they would have no part in his inheritance."

"Really?" Kathy replied. "And how do you know all this?"

"Oh, I'm sorry," Mrs. Fraser replied. "I don't suppose anyone ever told you that Mrs. Henderson is my cousin. She and I have always been good friends."

"No, no one ever told me," Kathy answered. "But I see that my parents are ready to go now. It was nice visiting with you."

Mrs. Fraser bobbed her head again. "It was a pleasure talking to you. I'll see you again sometime."

"Whew!" Kathy exclaimed as she plopped into the car. "I learned more about Matthew Henderson in the last half hour than I ever knew before. I tried to ask Mrs. Fraser about how he came to donate an expensive window to the church. But all she could talk about was how mean he was to his family and all that. In fact, she never even mentioned the window."

"Probably because she doesn't really remember it," Father spoke up. "All the things he did that were intended to impress people didn't really impress anyone. Because, after all, people will remember what kind of person he really was instead of what he tried to make them think he was."

With a wink in Kathy's direction, Jonathan started out, singing heartily: " 'Fading away like the stars of the morning, / Losing their light in the glorious sun— / Thus would we pass from the earth and its toiling, / Only remembered by what we have done.' "

As she joined in the chorus of that familiar hymn, Kathy thought about the words. Then a sobering thought silenced her for a minute. *I wonder,* she thought to herself. *What will people remember* me *by?*

21

The Preschool Class

"Oh, Marlene," Ruby began as the two met at the back of the church, "I've been wanting to tell you what Karen told me."

Marlene stepped out of the aisle to let some younger girls pass. As she did so, she thought quickly. *Ruby's daughter Karen is a student in my preschool Sunday school class.*

"No, no, it's nothing bad." Ruby chuckled. "I walked into the room as Karen was playing with her dolls the other day. She looked up and said to me, 'When I'm big, I want to teach Sunday school. And do you know what? I want to be a teacher just like Sister Marlene. She has the interestingest classes.' "

"That's nice," Marlene offered. "I enjoy teaching the children."

"We really appreciate your efforts with your class," Ruby went on. "We can see that Karen is getting more out of her Sunday school lessons than her older sister did at her age. I'll have to be going now, but I'd just like to tell you this yet: you must be doing a good job. Keep it up!"

Marlene watched Ruby follow her husband out through the front door. *So,* she thought, *Ruby and Peter think I'm doing a good job. Hmm.* She tucked the thought into a cubbyhole and turned to greet her cousin.

Later, as the family rode home from church, Marlene's brother Roger turned to her. "Did you know that the Sunday school reorganization meeting will be held this week?" he asked.

"No, I didn't."

"Would you like to know who is on the nominating committee?" he asked next.

"Sure," Marlene responded. "Probably won't make much difference to me anyhow."

"It will be the superintendent, of course, and one of the ministry. And the other two members will be John Decker and Peter Martin."

"Peter Martin?" Suddenly Marlene remembered what his wife had told her just that morning about her class of preschool children. "Keep it up," Ruby had added.

Marlene's thoughts raced all the rest of the way home. *I've really enjoyed teaching the preschool class. Surely, if Peter and his wife think I'm doing a good job, they'll ask me to teach for another year. Maybe they've already thought of asking me, and she just gave me a hint. I've been teaching two years now. Wouldn't it be interesting if I could teach that class three years in a row?*

And besides, her thoughts ran on, *since the class will be getting larger, surely they will want an experienced teacher for it. Not that I'm an expert,* she amended hastily. *But I know the children well by now, and they know me.*

The more Marlene thought about it, the more she convinced herself that the teaching job would be hers for another year. Her heart warmed within her as she imagined the happy looks of "her" children when she stood before them again.

In the bookstore on Tuesday afternoon, she caught herself looking for suitable stickers to use with the Sunday school memory verses. *Come now,* she scolded herself guiltily. *You don't even know yet if you have the job or not. Better leave them there until after Sunday.* But the longer she looked at the selection, the more attractive they seemed to become. A short time later, she walked out of the store with a pack of puppy stickers in the bag under her arm.

Wednesday evening, after prayer meeting, Marlene watched the members of the Sunday school nominating committee carefully. When not one of them came to talk to her, she slowly followed her brother to his car. *Must be they are going to phone those they want to ask,* she decided.

All the rest of that week, Marlene listened carefully whenever the telephone rang. Every day her hopes diminished. Finally on Saturday afternoon, she sat down to study her Sunday school lesson. "The last lesson in this year," she whispered. "That means tomorrow they'll announce the new teachers."

Like an electric shock, the thought shot through her: *They haven't asked me to teach again. If they haven't by now, they likely don't plan to.*

Turmoil boiled within Marlene. She folded her arms on her desk and rested her head on her wrists. Tears streamed onto the papers on the desk. When her mother came into the room fifteen minutes later with some folded laundry, Marlene was still motionless.

"Why, Marlene," her mother said softly, "can you tell me about it?" She pulled up a chair and sat beside the desk.

Marlene sat up and reached for a tissue. As her sobs subsided, she told her mother all about how badly she had wanted to teach the preschool class again and how she knew now that someone else would get the privilege. "I know it sounds very childish for a twenty-year-old," she concluded.

Mother looked thoughtful for a minute. "I think," she began, "that you have gotten your eyes on your own self-worth and have forgotten about esteeming others better than yourself.

"Don't get me wrong, Marlene. You are worth a lot," she said with a smile. "But there are other young girls who are worth just as much as you are and who probably can teach just as well as you can. I know you enjoyed teaching that class; maybe you let some pride come into your attitudes about it. I know you don't want to be selfish and claim the class as your very own, do you?"

Marlene shook her head. "No, I really don't."

"The committee may have decided it is time for you to step aside and let someone else have a turn," Mother continued softly. "That really doesn't matter. What does matter is that with pride in your heart regarding teaching, you would have crowded out the blessings God had in it for you. And besides, what would you have taught the children?"

Marlene pondered that for several minutes. Then she said, "Thank you, Mother. I think I see now what I was doing."

"You're welcome, Marlene."

As her mother got up to leave the room, Marlene dropped her head onto her desk again. "I'm sorry, Lord," she prayed. "I've failed a test again. Please forgive me. And help me to submit humbly to the decisions of those above me, without any pride in my own abilities."

The next morning, just after Sunday school, Marlene listened carefully as Brother Peter announced the names of the new teachers. " . . . and Becky Smith for preschool," he finished.

Marlene's heart sang within her as she realized that she could honestly rejoice with Becky instead of envying her. "Thank You, Lord," she breathed. "I couldn't have had the victory without Your grace."

22

Not Enough Cake

Delbert hung up the telephone with a clatter and returned to his half-eaten supper. Faith opened her eyes wide at his discomfort, but she knew that her husband would tell her what he thought without her asking him.

Sure enough, he cleared his throat and began. "That mission board," he sighed, "sure seems to need a lot of money. I tried to tell Brother Daniel that I put a tenth of my wages into the offering every week. I can't help it that the mission offering only comes once a month."

Faith swallowed another bite of bread. "A tenth?" she asked. "Is that all?"

"That is a tithe," Delbert pointed out. "In fact,

I'm being generous with them. I round it off in their favor when I write out my check."

"But only a tenth?" Faith repeated, frowning. "Couldn't we afford to give the mission board something more than that? Especially if they have a special need?"

"I know I make good wages there at Vizier Welding," Delbert admitted. "But we have all sorts of demands on our funds right now. And remember, we need to be saving up our money for the farm that we want to buy soon." He smiled fondly at his wife. "You agreed with me that we should try to live on a farm as soon as we can, didn't you?"

"I did," Faith agreed. "But this makes me feel greedy, somehow. If the mission board starts calling around and asking for funds, they must really need the money."

Delbert shifted himself in his chair. "I guess you're right. They do need money quite badly right now for that new house in Guatemala. But if I'm helping them already with my tithes, why do I need to finance this whole project?" He shook his head at the bowl she passed him. "No, thanks; I've had enough potatoes already."

Faith looked thoughtful as she rose to bring their dessert from the cupboard.

"Oh, good!" Delbert rejoiced. "Chocolate pudding cake! Still warm! My favorite!" He helped himself to two pieces and then poured milk on them in his dish. Faith smiled and shook her head when he offered her the milk pitcher. "That's right," he added, grinning. "I don't know how you learned to eat cake without milk."

They ate in companionable silence for a few minutes. Suddenly Faith cleared her throat and asked, "What if I wouldn't let you have any more of this cake?"

Delbert blinked. "What's up?" he asked. "What happens with the rest of it?"

Faith pointed to the hole they had made in the cake. "That's more than a tenth of the cake," she said. "Isn't that about enough for you?"

"For right now," Delbert agreed. "But I'll soon be hungry again. I might be able to eat another two pieces for a bedtime snack, if they're no bigger than these."

"I can't help that," Faith replied. "I'll be baking another cake next week. You can have some of that one."

"What will I eat from now until then?" Delbert wanted to know. "You know I like dessert with my meals. Especially in my lunch pail."

Faith nodded. "I know. But what if I could only afford to let you have this much of every cake I bake?" Her eyes twinkled at him.

Now Delbert looked astounded. "What will you

do with all the rest?" he asked.

Faith grinned. "Oh, there are lots of ways to use cake. I could eat some myself, of course. We're having a family gathering here soon, remember? That will take a lot of cake. And I could make lots of friends among the neighbors with that much cake. And I could . . . oh, I could do all kinds of things."

"So you're keeping nine-tenths of the cake for yourself? Wouldn't that be kind of greedy?" Delbert wondered.

Faith looked at him steadily. "Any more greedy than keeping back nine-tenths of a paycheck from the Lord?" she asked.

A light began to dawn on Delbert's face. After a bit, he said slowly, "You know, that does look greedy, doesn't it."

"Are you talking about money or cake now?" Faith asked, smiling.

Delbert was still thinking. "That does look greedy, doesn't it," he repeated. "A tithe is a tenth. I always thought . . ." His voice trailed off.

Faith waited. "Thought what?" she asked finally.

Delbert paused, and then he said, "I always thought I was doing my duty by giving the church a tenth of my paycheck. But it sure looks different when you're on the opposite end of things." He smiled at her. "One tenth looks like a very small part of a whole cake. Especially when it's all you get."

"Oh, you can have all you want," Faith replied. "But that will be my *offering* to you."

Delbert's eyes widened. "Tithes and offerings," he remarked. "I never thought about the difference before. The Bible commands us to bring in the tithes and offerings, and to give as the Lord has prospered us. Must be that God considers offerings separate from tithes?"

"I think so," Faith said. "I agree with you; it does look greedy of me to keep nine-tenths of the cake for myself, doesn't it."

"Especially when it's just as much mine as yours, right?" Delbert asked, grinning. Then he sobered. "I must admit I didn't realize as I should have that everything belongs to God. And really, He's promised to supply all our needs. From now on, I want to give more of my means to Him as He has prospered me and let Him do what He wants with it." He picked up his fork and poked it into a piece of cake. "Thank you, Faith, for this reminder. After supper I'll call Brother Daniel back. I've changed my perspective."

"You're welcome," Faith answered, her eyes twinkling again. "I'm glad. And you really, truly may have more cake anytime you want it. That's a promise."

23

Professor Johnson

Richard shifted the basket of tracts on his arm. Just then, the DON'T WALK light across the street changed to WALK, and he stepped off the curb and walked to the other side. He shivered in the damp September breeze. "Sure glad it's not so hot today," he whispered to himself. "At least the people here in the city have clothes on today."

Richard and several other men from his congregation had been walking up and down the streets of Brucefield since midmorning, handing out tracts to the people they met. This was Richard's first experience at tract distribution, and he felt exhilarated when he considered all the possibilities before him. Nearly half an hour before this, he and his uncle Jonathan had decided to take opposite sides of a street. Now Richard saw that he was nearing the end of the street and that his uncle was still a block behind him. So he decided to take advantage of the bench at the corner of the sidewalk. A short rest would feel good to his tired feet.

Before long, a well-dressed man settled down beside him. When Richard felt the stranger's keen eyes upon him, he looked up and smiled. "Would you like a Gospel paper, sir?" he asked, gathering several tracts from the top of his basket.

The man took one look at the tracts Richard offered him. "You can't sell me that one," he sneered. "I don't believe it anyway."

"But I'm not selling them," Richard protested. "I'm giving this to you as a gift because I love your soul."

"How do you know I have a soul?" the man countered. "I don't believe in things I can't see. But that's beside the point. What I want to know is: Do you really believe that bunk about Jesus coming again?"

Richard cleared his throat and looked down at the tracts in his hand. Only then did he notice the title of the top tract: *Jesus Is Coming—Perhaps Today.* "Yes," he began carefully, "I certainly do believe it."

"But how do you know?" the man asked.

"Well," Richard said, "He came as a baby to Bethlehem, and the angels announced His birth to the shepherds. And—"

The man waved his hand impatiently. "Oh, I know, I know. You Christians keep telling us that story, and so many people believe it that it must be at least partly true. But what I want to know is, How do you know your Jesus will come again, as you say He will?" He stopped and waited expectantly.

For an instant, Richard had the sickening feeling that this man was looking at him in the same way that a cat looks at a mouse in a corner. "Dear Father," he prayed hurriedly, "give me the words to speak. This man obviously thinks he's well informed."

Because Richard did not reply immediately, the man began again. "The world is getting better and better, isn't it? At least, nothing much has changed since, oh, hundreds of years ago. Unless you consider the area of technology, of course, which is getting better all the time."

"I beg to disagree," Richard said. "According to my father and my grandfather, the world is getting worse and worse all the time."

The man chuckled deep in his throat. "Your father and your grandfather," he scoffed. "How much do they know, after all? How old are you?"

"Eighteen."

"So you haven't really seen much yet. I presume your father and your grandfather colored a lot of your opinions regarding the Bible. Am I right?"

Richard nodded. "I, well, I've done a lot of studying on my own," he said. "But I will admit that they've taught me a lot and that I'm thankful for it. Why?"

The stranger turned on the bench and faced Richard squarely. "Why?" He spat the word. "Why? Why listen to the old folks, with all their old-fashioned ideas? If you do that, you'll never get ahead. How much of today's wonderful technology would you be acquainted with if you did everything as your father and your grandfather did? Not very much, I dare say."

Richard kept silent. In his mind, he was feeling uneasy. This smooth-tongued stranger nearly made him feel as if he had lost his balance and was grasping for a handhold somewhere. Richard treasured the solid Christian teachings he had received from his parents, but somehow they were starting to totter in front of this stranger's onslaught.

"Another thing," the stranger went on, "how would you know about Jesus' coming again if your forefathers hadn't told you about it?"

"I can read it in the Bible," Richard answered readily. "And the signs of His coming are everywhere, according to the Bible."

The stranger chuckled. "The Bible!" he exclaimed. "Always the Bible! How do you even know the Bible is true? How can you prove it wasn't invented by somebody to scare people into behaving?"

"It wasn't," Richard answered. "It—"

"Yes, but prove it," the stranger insisted. "I've studied it all out, and you can't prove that to me anymore. In fact, I've been studying human history, and you can't even prove to me that people are getting worse instead of better."

"I see," Richard agreed reluctantly. "You are right: if you are not willing to believe what the Bible says, I won't be able to prove anything to you."

"Of course you can't," the stranger declared. "Because you can't prove that it's true, first of all. And it is certain that you can't prove to me that Jesus is coming again. No one has ever seen Him coming yet, and I won't believe that He'll come until I see Him." He got up and dusted off his briefcase. "So long. I feel sorry for you and your old-fashioned ideas, but it was nice talking to you anyhow."

Richard stared after the retreating stranger. Suddenly he became aware of the noises of the

city again. He looked around and noticed that
Uncle Jonathan was walking across the street
toward him.

"How did it go for you?" Uncle Jonathan
asked. "I noticed you were speaking with Professor Johnson, from Fanshawe College. What
did he have to say?"

"Oh, Uncle Jonathan," Richard answered
impulsively. "How *can* we prove that Jesus is coming again? He tried to tell me we can't prove the
Bible is true either. I know in my heart that it is,
but he almost made me question it." Speaking rapidly, Richard related their conversation.

Uncle Jonathan smiled sympathetically. "I'm
sorry you had to run into such a person today," he
said softly. "You're so young yet. Professor Johnson is also our lawyer, and I know how he can talk.
However, did you tell him that the Bible talks
about people like him?"

"It does?" Richard asked, surprised. "I'm
ashamed to admit that he had me so rattled I
almost couldn't think of what the Bible says."

Uncle Jonathan nodded. "He knows how to do
that. But here"—he pulled a small New Testa-
ment out of his shirt pocket—"look at what Peter
says about people who don't believe that Jesus is
coming again." Uncle Jonathan's fingers rapidly
flipped pages until they stopped at 2 Peter 3.

" 'Knowing this first,' " he read aloud, " 'that there shall come in the last days scoffers, walking after their own lusts, and saying, Where is the promise of his coming? for since the fathers fell asleep, all things continue as they were from the beginning of the creation. For—' "

"That's exactly what he tried to tell me," Richard interrupted, "that things haven't changed. In fact, he was sure the world was getting better and better."

Uncle Jonathan paused. "That's what some people say," he agreed. "But listen. 'For this they willingly are ignorant of, that by the word of God the heavens were of old, and the earth standing out of the water and in the water: whereby the world that then was, being overflowed with water, perished: but the heavens and the earth, which are now, by the same word are kept in store, reserved unto fire against the day of judgment and perdition of ungodly men.' "

Richard listened carefully. When his uncle's voice stopped, his mind went back over what the professor had said. Then with a start, Richard realized that Uncle Jonathan was looking at him expectantly.

"Thank you, Uncle Jonathan," he managed to reply. "I never realized in this way before what those verses could mean."

"You're welcome, Richard," Uncle Jonathan replied warmly. "If you have any more questions, feel free to ask me on the way home. In the meantime, there's a multitude of people milling around us who need to know about Jesus' coming. Shall we go and tell them?"

24

"See You Later"

When the little silver bell tinkled above the bakery door, Mother looked up. "I think you'd better see what they want," she told Sharon. "I've got both hands sticky from dipping these cookies."

Sharon laid down her pastry brush and walked through the swinging door into the front part of her family's bakery. "Good morning, Mr. Humphrey," she greeted the customer. "I haven't seen you for quite a while. What can I get for you today?"

Mr. Humphrey grunted. "Not so much, not so much today. My missis, she wants me to bring three loaves of bread. Some of that honey oatmeal, please." He paused and surveyed the goods laid out in the showcase in front of him. "And some cinnamon rolls," he added. "She likes those with her coffee in the morning."

Sharon set his selections on the counter. "Here you are," she said. "May I get you anything else?"

"Hmm. I don't know. Well, maybe some of those Danish things." Mr. Humphrey pointed into the showcase. "They look good. Give me half a dozen of those."

"They taste good too," Sharon remarked as she piled six of the sweet rolls into a small box. "I like them quite well myself."

Mr. Humphrey nodded his head. "I believe you," he said. "I really do believe you, but I can't taste them anymore." At her look of surprise, he continued. "I have half my jaw made of plastic now. And most of the inside of my mouth is plastic too."

"Really?" Sharon could hardly understand that. "What did you do? I don't remember that you were in any accident recently."

"Got cancer," he stated flatly. "They cut it out and patched me up, but now I can't taste. All my food has to go through the baby-food grinder now," he added. "Do I look like a baby?" He chuckled, but his face did not look happy.

Sharon surveyed his large form. "Not really," she had to admit. She turned back to the cash register.

Just then Father came around the corner with an armful of fresh loaves for the shelf. "Did you say you had cancer?" he asked. "Is it all gone now?"

Mr. Humphrey smiled a crooked little smile. "No, it's not," he said quietly. "That's what scares me. I'm just thankful I can still eat. Some of my friends got cancer, and they're all gone already. So I'm just grateful I'm still alive."

Father set the loaves down one by one. "We know we'll all be leaving sometime," he stated. "If we are ready to die, we need not fear death."

Mr. Humphrey pulled out his billfold. "Seven-fifty, you say?" he addressed Sharon. "Here it is."

He picked up the bag of bread and turned to Father again. "Oh, I know," he said, suddenly bold. "I've got my contract with the undertaker all written out already. My funeral is all planned too. I have nothing more to do but die."

"There is something very important that everyone must do," Father said. "Have you prepared to face God, the judge, after death? Everyone must meet Him someday. Are you ready?"

"I'm ready to die," Mr. Humphrey insisted. "My funeral is all ready. Isn't that enough?"

"If your sins have been forgiven and your soul has been washed clean by the blood of Jesus Christ, it is enough," Father answered.

Mr. Humphrey stood up very straight. "Well,

I'm a good man," he said. "I don't drink or smoke or steal, and I'm faithful to my wife. I told you, I'm ready to die." He made a move toward the door. "See you later, friend. Good-bye."

Father watched him go. "Good-bye," he said. "I hope I *will* see you later—in the home of the redeemed."

Sharon, still standing by the cash register, watched the man as he stamped along the sidewalk. "You gave him something to think about," she remarked. "I wonder what he will do."

"I wonder too," Father said. "I feel I should visit him sometime soon and warn him again."

Father did visit Mr. Humphrey the next weekend. But he came back shaking his head. "The cancer is growing again, and fast," he told Mother and Sharon. "But he still insists he is ready to die. I'm afraid he will find out differently very soon. The end of life comes so quickly, and what then? Let's take this as a warning to be ready all the time."

25

"You Must Forgive"

After church, on Sunday morning, the youth girls soon found their way outside and into the spring sunshine. "God bless you, Bertha," Alice greeted her newly converted friend beside her in the circle. "It's good to be home again."

"Are you sure?" Bertha laughed. "I heard you had a good time over there at Mountain Dale."

"Oh, I did," Alice agreed. "But working as a hired girl when your sister has twins is not all fun either, even if I enjoyed it. I've never worked in a situation like that before."

Bertha nodded. "But you didn't have to stay with the babies all the time, did you?"

"Oh, pretty well," Alice answered. "They have

four children older than the twins, so we had a lot of things to do. That kept me quite busy."

"Four weeks seems like a long time," Leah remarked. "How could you stand it?"

"Oh, it wasn't that bad," Alice answered. "In fact, I enjoyed it so much I didn't think of the time very often. Besides, I've been home since Thursday, so it wasn't quite four weeks."

"And four weeks isn't very long," Bertha put in. "Sometimes people change a lot in less time than that." She gave Alice a knowing look.

Alice blinked. Bertha seemed to think she knew something serious. Whatever could it be?

"But so far from home," Leah insisted. "Why did your sister Helen and William have to move so far away anyhow?"

"It only takes two hours," Alice objected. "And we're glad the little mission in the mountains does so well. Aren't you?"

"I guess so," Leah admitted. "But it's—"

"That's not so far," Bertha said, interrupting. "My brother and his carpenter crew work in that area sometimes. In fact, they worked there last week, and he said he saw you there."

"Me?" Alice looked astonished. "Where did he see me?"

"Well," Bertha began, "you know he isn't a Christian anymore. While he and his crew walked from their job site to the hotel, they met you and another boy in a pickup."

Alice's mouth dropped open. A gasp ran around the circle.

Bertha paused. "At least he said the girl looked exactly like you. My brother wouldn't lie, would he? He said you had on a flashy pink dress and you had your hair puffed all over the place. Did he say the truth?"

"Most certainly not," Alice answered when she found her voice. "I did not go to town at all last week. I don't even own a pink dress, and why would I want to puff my hair like that? And who was I with?"

Bertha shrugged. "People do strange things sometimes when they go away from home. Why would my brother start telling lies like that?"

Alice swiftly scanned the circle of girls, noting the expressions on each face. Then she turned and stumbled across the parking lot through the tears that blinded her eyes.

She found Mother already in the car, waiting for Father and the younger boys to come too. "Why, Alice!" Mother exclaimed. "Can you tell me about your problem?"

"Oh, Mother," Alice burst out. "I counted them as my friends. Now they believe the story Bertha told them, and it isn't true!" She poured into

Mother's waiting ears the story she had just heard about herself. "I think she's jealous of me," Alice finished.

"Now, now," Mother disagreed. "I wouldn't say that. You'll have to forgive her, of course. And make sure you don't falsely accuse your sisters in Christ."

"But I don't see—" Alice began and then stopped when Father got into the car. She and Mother exchanged glances, and Alice was grateful for an understanding mother. She knew from former experience that Mother would likely tell Father about this struggle, and together they would pray for their daughter.

Immediately after washing the dishes, Alice picked up her Bible and started toward the door. "I'm going out to the orchard," she explained, at Mother's questioning glance. "I have to sort something out."

Mother smiled and nodded.

Alice settled herself into a comfortable position and opened her Bible. "Lord, what do You want me to do?" she whispered. "I don't really want to forgive Bertha at all. Do I need to?" She fanned the open pages of the Book in her lap.

Quietly the Holy Spirit touched her heart and whispered in her ear. "You must forgive," He said, echoing Mother's words. "Of course you must forgive."

"Do I have to?" Alice questioned.

" 'But if ye forgive not [others],' " the voice said, " 'neither will your Father forgive your trespasses.' "

Alice considered that for a bit. "I do want God to forgive my sins," she realized. "But it's so hard to forgive Bertha."

"Yes," the voice agreed. "Nevertheless, you must."

Then another voice demanded her attention. "You've never done anything as bad as what Bertha did," this voice stated. "So you don't need to forgive her just yet. Don't let her get away with spreading stories like that. That story is far from true, and you know it. It's not fair for you to have to take the blame in this case."

For some time, the battle raged in Alice's heart. On one side, a voice kept telling her, "It's not fair." And on the other side, the Spirit kept repeating, "You must forgive, of course." Alice knew in her heart which voice spoke the truth. "But it's so hard," her own self cried out.

Finally, she drew a deep breath. *I can't go on like this,* she decided. *I asked God what I should do, and I have not even looked in the Bible. Let me see, what verses can I find?* She looked down at her Bible and ran her finger down across the open pages. The words jumped out at her: "So likewise shall my heavenly Father do also unto you, if ye from your hearts forgive not every one his brother their trespasses."

Amazed, Alice lifted her eyes and looked up through the branches of the tree above her. "That almost sounds like a threat," she whispered to herself. She bowed her head again and read the rest of that familiar story about the servant who owed much and had his debt forgiven. Then, because of the servant's treatment of his fellow servant, his lord cast him into prison and delivered him to the tormentors.

Alice shivered when she came again to the verse that started, "So likewise . . ." Then she lowered her head still more, and a few tears squeezed out of her eyes. "Lord," she prayed, "I see it now. I need to forgive Bertha, even this great wickedness, if I want You to forgive me. And I do want You to forgive me, for I realize my own weakness so much." She paused. "I can't do it by myself, Lord," she went on. "But I claim Your grace in order to forgive her." Then, as peace unfathomable flooded her soul once more, Alice let out a deep sigh. "Thank You, Lord. Help me always to forgive so that I don't stop Your forgiveness from reaching me. Help me not to think of what Bertha did as a great wickedness."

After some time in meditation, Alice gathered

up her Bible and started toward the house. Mother met her at the door. "Bertha called," she told Alice. "She wants you to call her back right away."

"Bertha?" Alice felt a stab of fear in her heart. "I forgave her," she told Mother. "Truly I did. But must I be tested so soon?"

Mother nodded. "Go ahead and call her," she said, smiling. "She might surprise you."

Alice called. And as soon as Bertha heard Alice's voice, she started to apologize for what she had said. "I'm so sorry I repeated that silly story. How could you possibly stand there so calmly?"

Alice did not answer.

"You see, it's like this," Bertha explained. "After we came home, I started thinking about it a bit more. Didn't you say you came home from your sister's on Thursday?"

"Yes, I did," Alice answered.

"Well, my brother told me the story on Friday evening. I understood he saw you that day. Just a little bit ago, I checked with him, and he said, yes, he saw that couple on Friday. So it couldn't have been you. I'm so sorry." Her voice carried tears. "That was dreadfully wicked of me to believe something like that about my sister in Christ. Can you possibly forgive me, Alice?"

Alice drew a deep, shaky breath. "I already have," she assured Bertha. "Out in the orchard,

I found peace when I told God I would forgive you. But I thank you for calling anyway. Now we can face each other again with nothing between us."

"Thank you," Bertha answered softly. "I'll make sure the rest of the girls find out about this. And from now on, I will be very careful what kind of things I believe about people."

"Me too," Alice answered. "God bless you."

26

The Door That Opened

Robert Miller laid down his welding gun and lifted the helmet from his face. *Only thirty-seven more to go,* he calculated quickly. *Then I can start on my quota for Monday.* He scanned the row of welding stations on either side of him, taking note of the stacked parts behind each man. *Looks as if we're all making good headway today,* he remarked to himself. Then he picked up another pin foot and plunked it onto the tube in the jig in front of him.

Weld, flip the jig, weld, change parts, weld, flip the jig, weld, change parts. Gradually the pile of tubes on the skid beside Robert disappeared, only to appear on the other side of him with pin feet neatly welded onto each one. All around him, welders flashed and sputtered in the endless rhythm of a smoothly running production line.

When the buzzer rang for break time, Robert laid his gun down and sighed. The rhythm of production welding was becoming a welcome routine. Besides, he enjoyed working in this shop, even if he was the only Christian out of seventeen men. The place was clean and—what counted more— no one was allowed to smoke or use dirty language.

Beside him, Peter shrugged his apron off and flung it over his jig. "How do you like working Saturdays?" he asked as they headed for the lunchroom. "A bit different, eh?"

Robert nodded. "I don't really mind it though. We do have an obligation to help our boss finish this job on time."

Peter shrugged. "I can't help it if these customers are so fussy about schedules. But I sure don't mind being paid time and a half for a whole day. That adds up!"

"I agree," Robert answered. "And every little bit helps when you can hardly make ends meet. My wife and I—"

"Here's the boss," Peter interrupted, "coming over from his office for break time. Wonder what he wants?"

Robert did not answer. An uneasy knot formed in his stomach as he eyed Mr. Andrews standing beside the coffeepot. Mr. Andrews rarely joined his men at the lunch table; when he did, he usually had an announcement to make. Robert could think of only one announcement that would need to be made on a Saturday afternoon when they were hurrying to finish a job.

Sure enough, he did not have long to wait. Mr. Andrews cleared his throat, and the babble around the table became quiet. "Boys," he began, "as you all know, we're going to be pushed for time to get these racks ready to ship by Wednesday."

Greg, the foreman, nodded his head and looked around the table. "You're doing very well," he said, "but we're still a bit behind schedule, and lost time is hard to make up."

"That's right," Mr. Andrews added. "Since the deadline is so close upon us, and we still have almost a whole day's work to make up, I'm going to ask all of you to come back tomorrow." He scanned the faces turned up to his, and then added, "I know some of you won't like this, but consider it a sacrifice in order to keep your job."

"What do you mean by that?" someone asked.

"Just what I said. If I lose the business because of a late shipment, you'll lose your jobs for sure. So if you're not willing to hang in here and help to finish this rack order on time, you'll lose your job anyway."

Robert fought to control the panic that welled up inside him. He licked his lips carefully. "Do you intend to say," he began, and his voice sounded strangely unfamiliar, "that if we don't come in tomorrow, which is Sunday, we might as well not come back?"

Mr. Andrews shifted as if he were suddenly uncomfortable. "That's what I said," he answered.

"Oh."

"That goes for all of you," Mr. Andrews added quickly. "And that's all I've got to say right now." He cleared his throat again and returned to his office.

Robert watched Mr. Andrews disappear through the door, and his heart tumbled. Under no conditions would he think of coming in to work on a Sunday. He esteemed the Lord's Day too highly for such a thing. On the other hand, he could already see Amy's face when he told her that he no longer had a job. She would be disappointed, of course, but she would understand. But what about the creditors? Robert sighed and followed the rest of the workers back to their stations.

When the buzzer sounded for the end of the shift, Robert turned off his welder with a heavy heart. Although he dreaded the task ahead of him, he knew that he must go ahead with it. Sure enough, Mr. Andrews was still in his office. When

Mr. Andrews looked up from his desk, Robert got the distinct impression that he had expected him.

"Yes, what can I do for you?"

Robert took a deep breath. "I . . . I'm here to tell you that I cannot come tomorrow." There, it was out.

"I see." Mr. Andrews nodded. "You realize that such an action will terminate your employment at Form-Rite?"

"I realize that. But I feel that I cannot dishonor my Lord by failing to keep the Lord's Day holy unto Him."

Mr. Andrews opened his mouth and then closed it again. "Couldn't you worship God here?" he wondered. "I wouldn't mind letting you have an hour or so to do whatever you need to do."

"No." Robert shook his head. "We are told in Hebrews not to forsake the assembling of ourselves together with others to worship God."

"Very well then," Mr. Andrews replied. "You may expect your check and your severance papers in the mail next week."

That evening, when Robert stepped into the house, Amy looked up. "What's the matter?" she asked over the happy squeals of their two children. "You don't look very excited."

"I'm not," Robert said grimly as he picked up baby Katherine. "I guess I'll have to start looking for a job again on Monday morning."

Amy gasped. "What do you mean, look for a job? You haven't even worked at Form-Rite for six months yet. What happened?"

Robert sat down. "Let's eat supper first, and then I'll tell you all about it."

As he had expected, the news surprised Amy. However, she was not visibly disappointed. "Always stand up for God," she said, "and He will bless you for it." She paused, thinking fast. "We'll manage," she declared briskly. "The garden is coming in now, and I have lots of beans left from last year. And besides, God never closes one door but that He opens a better one somewhere."

Robert smiled. "I wish I could believe that," he said. "Right now I can't see anything but a wall. A wall with no doors."

It was nearly three weeks later when Robert came home dejected once again. "I've exhausted all the leads I've found," he told Amy. "It seems as if no one wants to hire right now. Even the feed mill said they have all the help they need. In fact, several people today talked of laying off some of their workers instead of hiring more."

Amy smiled sympathetically. "God is going to open a door somewhere," she reminded him. "All you have to do is find it."

"Find it," Robert repeated after her. "That's

the hard part. I don't even know where to look."

"You'll find it somewhere," Amy said softly. "But lunch is ready now. Let's eat before the chili gets cold. Oh, by the way, a man called today and would like you to call him back." She pulled a slip of paper from under the refrigerator magnet and handed it to him.

"Dennis Lemanski," Robert read aloud. He tucked the paper into his shirt pocket and picked up baby Katherine. "Who is this man, and what does he want?"

"He didn't say," Amy answered as she ladled soup into a serving bowl. "But he made it sound urgent that you call him today yet. You can wait until after lunch though, can't you?"

"I suppose. Here, Bruce, let me help you onto the chair."

By the time Robert was ready to call Dennis Lemanski, he was nearly consumed with curiosity. He had never heard the name before. What could a total stranger want that was so urgent? Very carefully he dialed the number that Amy had given him.

"Lemanski's Fine Furniture," said the cultured female voice at the other end of the line. "May I help you?"

"Yes, I would like to speak to Dennis Lemanski, please."

"Just a minute."

"This is Dennis. How may I help you?"

"Dennis, this is Robert Miller calling. I have a message here that you would like to speak to me."

"Oh, yes, Robert. Have you found a job yet?"

Astonished, Robert nearly dropped the telephone on the desk. "No, I haven't," he managed to reply.

The man on the telephone paused. "Robert," he began, "I've never done this before, but I have a feeling I'm doing the right thing. I am looking for a reliable bookkeeper. Would you consider the position?"

"I certainly would like to know more about it," Robert told him, "as long as I don't have to work on Sundays."

"I know," Dennis answered. Then before Robert could ask him to explain, he went on, speaking quickly. "As I said, I am looking for a bookkeeper. I need someone honest and reliable, someone I can trust to take care of my financial paperwork for me. I asked Mr. Andrews at Form-Rite if he knew of anyone he could recommend, and he recommended you."

"Me?" Robert asked, more astonished now than ever.

"Yes, you. He said—and I agree with him—that anyone who is willing to lose his job on a matter of principle would certainly have the qualifications I need."

Robert paused. This was almost more than he could comprehend. "But," he said, "how do you know I can even take care of a set of books?"

"You've had some experience, haven't you? According to your records at Form-Rite, you've taken a bookkeeping course. Is that correct?"

"Yes, it is," Robert had to agree. "I've been doing my own books here; but other than that, I have never handled a complete set of books. Would that be a problem to you?"

"No problem at all," Mr. Lemanski answered. "I'd be willing to train you on the job, if need be. As I said, all I need is an honest man, one I can trust. I'd be glad to pay you . . ." And he named a sum that made Robert smile. "How soon can you come? Would tomorrow morning be too soon?"

Robert thought fast. "Yes, I could come tomorrow morning. But how do I find your place?"

Mr. Lemanski chuckled. "Of course. I nearly forgot that we've never met. Now let's see. You take Route 35 to Orangeville . . ."

Several minutes later, when Robert hung up the telephone, Amy turned from where she was washing dishes. "That was interesting," she said. "Now what did he want?"

Robert stepped across the kitchen and leaned

against the counter beside the sink. "I have another job, starting tomorrow morning," he announced. "And guess what, Amy. The wages will be a bit higher than what I was earning at Form-Rite, with potential increase if things work out satisfactorily. And I didn't even have to ask for this one."

Amy beamed at him. "What did I tell you?" she asked with a playful smile. "God did open a door, and a better one at that. Shall we thank Him right away?"

27

The Galaxy Market

When Nancy heard Aunt Gertrude grunt, her rag stopped going in circles on the bedroom ceiling. She looked down from her perch on a chair. "Here, let me help you move that dresser," she offered quickly. "I'm here to help you houseclean today, and you know you shouldn't be hauling heavy furniture around with such a sore back."

Aunt Gertrude smiled widely as she straightened her back. "Now that is what I call good neighbors!" she said. "Not only did you offer to help an old bones like me with my cleaning, but you don't even allow me to work hard. Yes, I could use your help; Roy's dresser is heavier than I expected it to be."

"All right, here I come." Nancy let her rag drop into the pail of soapy water on the floor; then she hopped off her chair and squeezed past the bed. As she pushed the dresser back against the wall, a picture fell off and tumbled to the floor. Nancy picked it up and stared, astonished, at the brilliantly painted, short-haired girl who stared back at her.

"Who's that?" Nancy asked, holding the picture so that Aunt Gertrude could see. "That's not Roy's girlfriend, is it?"

Aunt Gertrude sighed. "I'm afraid it is," she answered. "Roy seems determined to go his own way, no matter what Jonathan or I tell him. He has a lot to do with the Restock boys, and they certainly are not good company for him. You've seen his new car, haven't you?"

"Yes, I have," Nancy said, wringing out her rag again. "And I can't see what is so good about a bright red sports car."

"I know you Mennonites don't drive such cars," Aunt Gertrude said. "You don't do many other things that we do, and I respect you for it." She leaned against the dresser. "We consider ourselves good people, Jonathan and I. But our son, Roy, . . ." She sighed and shook her head. "Our son, Roy, is another stripe altogether. But, as Jonathan says, he's not really a bad boy. We've just got to let him sow his wild oats, and maybe someday he'll settle down."

Maybe someday, Nancy thought to herself as she continued washing the ceiling. *But more likely, never.* Her heart ached for the sorrows that her uncle Jonathan had brought upon himself when he had turned his back upon his Christian heritage. Deaf to the pleas of his father and blind to the tears of his mother, he had joined the army in his youth. After several years, he had returned and married Gertrude, a girl from the city. Now Gertrude, stricken with arthritis, tried vainly to keep house and control their teenage Roy while Jonathan spent many long days driving a delivery truck. Nancy and her family lived nearby and often came to help Gertrude for a day or so.

Nancy hopped off the chair again and picked a cloth from the box by the door. "I'll wipe the walls now," she told Aunt Gertrude. "Then we'll be nearly done with this room. Do you want to start another room today?"

Aunt Gertrude fetched another cloth and went around the room, dusting everything as she went. "No," she said finally, "I think I will let you go home early today so that I can lie down and rest awhile before suppertime. My back doesn't take as much in a day as it used to."

"That is fine with me," Nancy answered cheerfully. "When I'm done here, I'll help you push everything back into place. And then I'll only need to put the bucket and stuff away."

A short time later, Aunt Gertrude sighed deeply. "Thank you very much for your help," she told Nancy. "I really appreciate your coming over like this. Now I'll have time to rest for about an hour before I need to make supper."

"You're welcome," Nancy answered. "I hope your back feels better by tomorrow." Then she picked up the bucket at her feet and stepped over into the laundry room.

Just as the last suds disappeared down the drain in the laundry tub, cousin Roy came in to hang up his coat. He raised his eyebrows when he saw what she was doing.

"Oh, you're done already?" he asked. "Then you'll have time to run to town for me yet before you go home. It's only two miles, you know."

Nancy turned and faced him warily. "What do you want me to do?"

"Come here." He beckoned to her as he stepped toward the kitchen. From the clutter on the table, he pulled out a brilliant pink flyer. "Here, see this," he said, pointing. "The Galaxy Market is selling milk for only two-eighty-nine a gallon. I want you to get some for me."

Nancy leaned closer. At the bottom of the page, in very small letters, she could read "Limit, three per family purchase."

"What about that?" she asked, pointing to the fine print.

"I've already got my limit of three," Roy told her. "And now I want you to get three more for me. I can freeze them so they won't turn sour. Think of it, Nancy, that's a savings of forty cents a gallon. You don't often see stuff like that around here."

"I know." Nancy took a deep breath. The Galaxy Market! She knew exactly where it stood in town. Shelves full of videos lined the walls, and indecent movie posters stared from every window. The very thought of entering that place gave her a feeling of disgust. "Lord, give me wisdom," she prayed quickly. "Don't let me yield to this."

Aloud she said, "I didn't know they sold milk. How does that fit in with the rest of their merchandise?"

"It doesn't," Roy said, his eyes searching her face. "They do things like that to get more customers into their store."

Nancy met his gaze calmly. "Well, it won't work on me," she told him. "I have no intention of going into that place, even if it's only for milk."

"Aw, come on, Nancy," Roy begged. "Be a good girl and go for me. If the boys in there wouldn't know me so well, I'd just go again myself. But I can't, because they know that I've already got my three gallons. Can't you do this for me? Please?"

Nancy shook her head.

"Not even if I let you have the dollar-twenty I'd save?" Roy asked. "I'd even pay you whatever you ask, just for doing it for me."

Still Nancy shook her head.

"Nancy, listen to me," Roy begged. "I'll let you have the dollar-twenty I'd save, and I'll even pay you five dollars more if you will go and get that milk for me."

For an instant, Nancy wavered in her resolve. "Save your money," she said finally. "I'm not interested in it."

"Not even if I let you drive my car over there? That way you wouldn't even waste any of your precious gas." Roy nearly sneered when he said that.

Nancy was not sure, but she thought she detected a gleam of triumph in his eyes. "That I will not do," she told him firmly. "Not only will I not set my foot inside that evil place, but I also refuse to drive that red Corvette that you call your car. Now, if you'll excuse me, I must be going home."

Roy watched as she put on her coat and picked up her purse. "Go home then," he answered finally. "And think about my offer. If you happen to change your mind before Friday evening, just call me right away. This special is good until then, and my offer stands as long as the special does."

Without answering, Nancy turned on her heel and headed for the door. In the entryway, she paused to slip into her boots, and then she skipped down the steps.

Just as she was ready to hop into her car, she remembered, *Oh, my gloves! I left them drying on the radiator in the kitchen.* Reluctantly she went inside again, leaving her boots at the door.

As she walked through the kitchen in her stocking feet, she heard someone say her name. Curious, she paused to listen.

Roy was sitting at the desk, speaking on the telephone. "She's not coming, Hank," he said. "So you might as well quit waiting for her and go on home." Roy leaned back in his chair, and Nancy could hear the echoes of someone's loud talk in the receiver that he held.

"Hank, I told you it wouldn't work," Roy went on, "but you insisted that I had to try, so I did a good job of it. I even offered her five dollars if she'd do it, but she refused, just like I expected she would. You know what, Hank? I would have been surprised if she'd have gone into that Galaxy Market." He drummed his fingers on the desk, listening. Then he said, "No, Hank, she's a good girl. Let's leave her alone after this, okay? You know that's not a good place for Christians to spend time in anyway."

Soberly Nancy tiptoed to the doorway and slipped into her boots. Soberly she got into her car and started it. Then she sat for a moment, thinking. *Just think,* she told herself, *Roy knew all along that I shouldn't go there. In fact, he didn't even expect me to go. If I had consented, he would have lost a lot of his respect for me, and I would have placed myself in the hands of his evil buddies.* A shudder passed through her. "Thank You, Father," she prayed aloud as she shifted gears, "for helping me through this temptation. By myself, I couldn't have made it. Help me to remember that those around me know more than I think they do about what I should or shouldn't be doing. And don't let me ever disappoint them."

Publisher's note: We are glad that Nancy did not yield to the temptation that she faced. However, we would recommend that our young girls not work in homes where they may face such temptations, including homes of apostate relatives.

28

A Great Awakening

"I wish you wouldn't need to go, James," Rhoda began as she watched him struggle into his coat. "You've barely come home, and now you must leave again. Besides, it's foggy this morning."

"I know," James agreed as he zipped up his jacket. "I don't really like it either. But someone has to make this early-morning delivery every day, and it might as well be me. You know that we badly need the extra money right now."

"Not as badly as we need you," Rhoda returned. "You know I've told you that before."

But James wasn't finished talking yet. "The boss pays me well," he went on, "even if he insists that I do a full day's work after I come back. And he says it's still cheaper than sending the parts down to the factory by commercial carrier."

"Wouldn't it be possible to make enough parts ahead that you'd only need to deliver them every other day?" Rhoda asked. "That would give you a breather, at least."

"Can't do that," James told her as he stamped into his boots. "That factory needs so many parts that it keeps us hopping to make one day's worth, let alone two days'. And they have to be delivered every day, or the production line would stop. You know we can't afford that."

"I know," Rhoda sighed. "But I still wish you'd be home more of the time. The children hardly see you anymore."

James reached for his lunch box. As he turned to go, he patted her shoulder. "Kiss them for me when they get up," he said, smiling. "I'll see you again at seven o'clock tonight, Lord willing." And then he was gone into the misty darkness.

Rhoda watched the lights of the pickup disappear into the fog. She sighed again as she looked at the clock over the kitchen sink. "Four-thirty," she remarked to no one in particular. "I may as well go back to bed again until the children wake up. These early mornings have a way of making the day seem extra long and tiresome."

When Donald and Kathy awoke several hours

later, they bounced out of bed enthusiastically. "Father home today?" three-year-old Donald asked eagerly. "Can we play 'boo'?"

"No, Donald," Rhoda told him and cringed as the light died in his eyes. "Father had to leave early again. But maybe Mother can play 'boo' with you." She knew how dearly he loved to play the game that he and his younger sister had invented.

As she and the children ate breakfast, Rhoda mentally planned her day. *I'd better do some washing if the sun shines this morning,* she planned. *Oh, no, I forgot to tell James that the washer doesn't work. Well, maybe I'll bake bread then. Donald would be delighted to help with that.*

She smiled at Kathy, and the child rewarded her with a sunny smile in return. *Such dears,* Rhoda reflected. *It's a shame that James can't see more of them. Before we know it, they'll be grown up.*

The ringing of the telephone interrupted her thoughts. Quickly she went to answer it.

"Rhoda," the voice at the other end said soberly, and she recognized it as James's voice. A stab went through her, and she clutched the telephone tightly.

"Yes, dear," she managed to reply.

"Rhoda," he began again, "I've had a little accident."

"Oh," Rhoda gasped. "What happened? Is anyone hurt? Are you all right?"

"No one's hurt," he replied, still sober. "No one else was even involved. I was tired, and looking at the fog made me very sleepy. Then I fell asleep and rolled over in the ditch. Now the truck is totaled, and I have a headache. Could you come and pick me up and bring me home?"

"Of course, James. Where are you now?"

He sighed, as if from relief. Rhoda could hear his voice tremble as he answered, "I'm here, at the shop. The accident happened on my way back, less than a mile from here. After the police officer was finished with me, he brought me over here. But my boss said I could have today off, and I'm glad."

"I can be there in about half an hour," Rhoda returned, planning quickly. "But what about the truck?"

"I've already asked my brother to tow it to his place this afternoon," James told her. "I'm hoping we can salvage the engine out of it. Just come over here right away, please. And be careful; it's still foggy in some places."

When she turned from the telephone, Rhoda caught up one of the children on each arm and carried them to the bathroom. As she washed their faces, she answered their questions. "No; Father is okay. . . . No, I don't know what happened. . . . Yes, we are going to see him."

This last statement brought squeals of joy from them, and when she set them down, Donald ran for their coats. He liked nothing better than a ride in the car, and an early-morning ride would be a special treat.

As she left the house, Rhoda noticed the dishes still sitting on the breakfast table. *Oh, well, I'll do them after I get back,* she told herself.

Rhoda tried to drive carefully as she drove to where James waited. Try as she might, she could not forget the soberness in his voice or the way his voice had quavered uncertainly. It was so unlike his confident, carefree way, and she could not decide what to make of it. Did it mean that he was trying to decide something? Or was he simply so shaken from the accident? Rhoda did not know. But she did know that fifteen miles had never seemed as long as it did then.

Finally, Rhoda arrived at the place where James worked. To her surprise, he was walking up and down in front of the building. When he saw her, he came quickly and slipped into the passenger's seat beside her. "You drive," he said huskily, in answer to her raised eyebrows. "I don't feel able to right now." He touched the left side of his forehead gingerly. "This bump is growing fast. Let's go home and get some ice on it."

Obediently, Rhoda turned the car around and

started back out the driveway. "Turn left first," James instructed her then. "I want to get the keys out of the truck yet. And maybe you'll want to see it?"

That sounded more like a statement than a question, and Rhoda swallowed hard. While she did not look forward to seeing their own pickup smashed, the idea did hold a certain fascination.

By the time she had decided that, they were there. Rhoda brought the car to a stop in front of a mass of twisted metal and shattered glass in the ditch. Then she gasped as her mind comprehended the fact that this pile was the remains of their pickup.

Rhoda stared at the pile in the ditch. She could not understand how anyone could have come out of that pickup alive. Yet, beside her sat her husband, with only a bump on his head and not even a scratch anywhere on him.

James got out of the car, and Rhoda slid out to join him. As they stood surveying the wreck, another car pulled up behind them. A lady came over and stood beside Rhoda.

"You are the fellow who was driving this pickup when it smashed, aren't you?" the lady asked James.

"Why, yes, I am," James answered, astonished. "How did you know?"

"Because you almost hit me head-on before you went into the ditch," the lady explained matter-of-factly. "I was taking my children and my sister's children to their grandmother for the day. When I saw you coming toward me in my lane, I blinked my lights and honked my horn. But you apparently didn't hear, so I ended up going over into the lane where you should have been. By that time you were so close that you only missed the front corner of my car by several inches. Was I scared! In fact, I'm still shaking from it."

Rhoda gasped and felt weak all over. She looked at James. His face was white, and his bruise showed up bright blue against the paleness. He did not say anything, so the lady went on. "I'm on my way home again now, and when I saw you here, I decided to stop. I thought maybe you'd like to know about it."

"Thank you for telling us," James said finally. "What do I owe you for your scare?"

"Oh, nothing, nothing," the lady said quickly. "I'm just glad that nothing more serious happened to me. And I suppose you had your truck insured, so you won't really have a loss either."

"No, we do not have insurance," James told her. "We feel we should trust the Lord to provide for us."

The woman looked at him strangely. "Well, to

each his own," she said finally. "I must be going now. See you later." Her heels clicked on the pavement as she stepped back to her car. Then she was gone.

James nearly staggered as he walked to the car again. "Are you going to be all right?" Rhoda asked him, concerned. "Should I take you to Dr. Owens for a checkup after all?"

"No, don't bother," James said, speaking slowly. "I just need a little time to think."

Donald and Kathy watched in awe as their tall, strong father carefully settled into his seat. He laid his head back on the seat, an expression of pain on his pale face. All the way home, he did not say a word, and Rhoda did not ask him any questions.

When they arrived at home, James was still quiet, and Rhoda marveled that the children were quiet as well. Slowly James laid himself down on the sofa. Rhoda prepared an ice pack for his head and brought it to him. "Ah," he sighed gratefully, "that makes it feel better already."

"You just rest now," Rhoda said as she plumped up a pillow for him. "There's nothing so important to do around here that you can't rest until you feel better." She gave the children their coloring books, and then she started washing the dishes.

Quite a while later, James suddenly sat up. "I wish we'd asked that lady what her name was," he said. "We might want to thank her for changing my mind."

Rhoda dried her hands and came to sit on a chair beside him. "Thank her?" she asked, puzzled. "For changing your mind? Whatever from? You barely even saw her."

"I know," James said. "But I've been doing some thinking. Can you guess what about?"

Rhoda sat still. She knew that James was aware of her dislike for his long hours of work. But she was afraid to ask if he was thinking about that, for fear she would be wrong. She need not have worried, however.

"I've decided it isn't worth it," James explained when she did not answer. "Trying to do so much work, that is. I know I fell asleep while driving this morning because I've been too tired lately from putting in such long days. Just think, Rhoda. I could easily have killed that lady and her children if I had hit them head-on. Or I could have been killed myself when the truck rolled over."

Rhoda shuddered. "I know, James. But I'm thankful you weren't."

"I am too," he agreed. He looked at Donald, still playing with his coloring book and crayons. "God has been speaking to me about what I've been doing and about what I said to that lady there beside the wreck."

"What was that?"

"I told her that we should trust the Lord to provide for us. At the time, I didn't think about what it means. But now I've come to the conclusion that if I really believe that God will provide for us, I won't need to ruin my health, and maybe my family as well, just to make a little more money. He's been telling me that if we are truly His, He will see that we are taken care of. So we are only running a useless rat race when we try to provide for ourselves without His help. Don't you think so, Rhoda?"

"Why, yes," Rhoda said, and tears threatened to spill onto her cheeks. "I've often thought the same thing. But you're not going to quit your job now, are you?"

"No, I don't think so," James said slowly. "My boss has been offering me a position at a welding station. That would be one nine-hour shift per day, starting at eight o'clock in the morning."

"Why don't you take it?" Rhoda asked. "It would be so nice to have you home earlier in the evenings and later in the mornings. Why," she added wistfully, "the children hardly know what family life is like anymore."

"The pay wouldn't be quite as much as it is now," James explained, "since the hours would not be as long."

"I'm sure we could get along fine on a little bit less," Rhoda told him quickly. "I'd be only too glad to try a little harder to save money if it would mean you'd be home more of the time."

James regarded her carefully. "A week ago I wouldn't have done such a thing," he said. "But somehow a smaller paycheck doesn't seem so terrible to me anymore. I had my eyes opened this morning to the foolishness of my own thinking." He sat thoughtfully for a minute, rubbing the ice over his forehead.

"Yes," he said finally, "that is what I will do. I will trust the Lord more fully from now on and behave myself a little more sensibly. I will call my boss today and ask him to get someone else to make the early-morning delivery, starting tomorrow. And then I will start that welding in a day or so, after my eye isn't so swollen anymore. That would mean I could be at home for a proper breakfast and supper. Then, among other things, we can start having a proper family worship again, for a change.

"And guess what, Rhoda. Now that I've decided that, I don't feel one bit bad about it. Do you think that's because it's the right decision?"

Rhoda nodded, too choked to speak. But the light in her eyes told James all that he needed to know.

29

The Whole Truth

An early-summer sun slanted through the window, casting its light on two young people, conversing as they finished their supper. An observer would have noticed that the brother and sister seemed to be having a disagreement.

"That I don't believe," Philip declared, pushing back his plate. "I don't see how it could be possible."

Dorcas stood up and gathered the plates and cups. "Oh, but it could be," she insisted. "Nancy said her brother-in-law heard it at work, and he's sure it was correct."

Philip frowned. "I still don't believe it," he said. "That story about Brother Larry Weaver just doesn't sound like anything he would do. Can't you give your brother in Christ the benefit of the doubt? At least until you find out the whole truth?"

"But it is the truth," Dorcas argued. "James wouldn't tell lies, would he?" She picked up the pile of dishes and took it over to the sink.

"No, I don't expect he would," Philip agreed. "But look. All you really know for sure is that the Sonco Metals truck driver says he saw Brother Larry pull out of the parking lot at the liquor store in the city. That doesn't prove a thing, in my mind. How can Nancy go by that and insist that Brother Larry has started drinking? Next thing you know, she'll have him a drunk."

Dorcas grinned. "No, she won't."

"I don't see why not," Philip replied. "But here, let me help you wash those dishes tonight. My chores are all done outside, and Father didn't give me anything extra to do while he and Mother are at that meeting."

Dorcas smiled at her brother. "Then I know what we should do," she said. "Let's finish here quickly and go and visit James and Loretta and check out that story. After all, I have to admit I do find it hard to believe that Brother Larry would shop at the liquor store."

Philip picked up a tea towel. "Better yet," he

answered, "let's just go on over to his house and ask Brother Larry himself."

"Ask Brother Larry himself?" Dorcas squeaked. "I can't do that!"

"Why not?" Philip wanted to know. "You had no problem repeating that silly story to me, and who knows how many of your friends have heard it by now. Yes, that's exactly what we'll do. Brother Larry often says he gets lonely—an old, widowed brother living all by himself like that. And if your courage fails you, or if your voice should give out suddenly"—he grinned down at his sister—"why, then I'll just ask Brother Larry myself. I'm not afraid of him, and I'm sure you're not either."

Dorcas examined the kettle in her dishwater as she scrubbed it. "Well," she said finally, "perhaps not really afraid. But it'll make me look foolish, won't it, if I have to ask him about what he did last Friday afternoon?"

"Not any more than when you're repeating a story that you don't know is true," Philip pointed out. "And even if it was true, you shouldn't go around telling things like that. You know that, don't you?"

Dorcas had no answer to his question. She pulled the plug and watched as her dishwater swooshed down the drain.

"Pleasant evening for a visit," Brother Larry

greeted the two young people at his door a short time later. "I just made me some popcorn and lemonade, and you're welcome to enjoy it with me. Here, we can relax out here on the porch on such a balmy evening."

Philip and Brother Larry settled into the two chairs, and Dorcas made herself comfortable on the porch swing. For a time, conversation flowed freely as the two men caught up on the week's events.

As he sipped his lemonade in the twilight, Philip casually asked, "So I hear you must have been in the city last Friday afternoon?"

Brother Larry thought for a moment. "Yes, I had to go and fetch another load of feed for my bunnies," he said. "Only one place in the city sells the right kind, and that is at the top end of Wellington Avenue."

"Is it true, then," Philip asked, with a glance in Dorcas's direction, "that somebody saw you coming out of the driveway of the liquor store last Friday evening?"

Brother Larry chuckled. "I wonder where he was, and what all else he saw," he remarked.

"So it is true?" Philip asked, and his voice sounded dismayed.

"Oh, sure it's true," Brother Larry answered readily. "But I still wonder where that person was and what all else he saw. Seems to me they must have had really selective vision somehow."

Dorcas choked back a cry at the matter-of-fact tone of Brother Larry's voice. Had he no remorse?

Philip helped himself to another handful of popcorn. "Selective vision?" he prodded.

"Oh, yes, in a mighty way indeed," Brother Larry answered. He poured himself a drink from the pitcher and calmly drank down the whole glassful. Then he added, "Beats me how anybody could have seen me coming out of that driveway without seeing the rest of the story."

By this time Dorcas was nearly in tears. So she almost didn't hear when Brother Larry went on. "You see, there'd been an accident right in front of the liquor store, and the whole rush-hour traffic on a Friday afternoon had to cut across in the back alleyway and come out on the other side of the liquor store back onto the street. Made a big mess, that it did. I was in that stream of traffic. That's all there is to the story."

"That's all?" Philip echoed, his voice extra loud in the gathering darkness.

"That's all," Brother Larry replied. "Here, have some more lemonade?"

For a long time, the two young people sat in silence, digesting this new version. A cow mooed in the distance, and several fireflies blinked on the lawn. A dog barked at the neighbor's, and far away the whistle of a train echoed into the sunset.

Finally Dorcas stood to her feet and stepped over to stand in front of the two men. "Thank you, Brother Larry," she said. "I've learned a tremendous lesson tonight. I'm sorry that I believed someone who told me you'd been shopping at that liquor store, and who even embellished that story with your motives for doing so. I hope that after this I will be more careful."

Brother Larry grinned widely as he and Philip stood to their feet as well. "Sure, sure," he said amiably. "We all need reminders sometimes. Thank you for coming, and I hope you can sleep better now."

"I will," Dorcas promised.

"Thank *you*," Philip said as he shook Brother Larry's hand. "I don't think I'll forget this evening right away. Come, Dorcas, we must be going home now."

On the way home, Philip could not suppress his grin. "Now do you see what I mean?" he demanded. "Even though the story that you had— the part of the story that you *really* had, I mean— was true, it certainly was not the whole truth. After this, I hope we'll all be more careful of the kinds of things we believe and pass on."

"I hope so too," Dorcas agreed fervently.

30

There Is a Difference

"Lunchtime," Kelvin announced, picking up the lunch box on the counter. "Let's eat before too many more customers come around."

Rosalie grinned at her brother, knowing his appetite. "Just let me wrap Mrs. Frank's sausage order yet, and then I'll be ready," she replied. "Did you tell George and Theresa that we're going to lunch?"

Kelvin shook his head and stepped to the opposite end of the long meat cooler. There George Lanning and his wife relaxed for a moment after the hectic rush of another morning at the farmers' market.

"Brought your own lunch today?" George

teased. "I told you you'd get tired of hamburgers twice a week. Sure, take your time for lunch. We're not so busy right now."

"Thank you," Kelvin replied. "We'll go to those tables over there. Then we can see if you get too rushed, and come back if you need us."

Kelvin and his sister had barely settled themselves when they saw him. The big man who strode toward them had determination written all over his face. And when he settled himself into the chair across the table from them, Rosalie heard the chair's creaking protest.

Over the hubbub of the marketplace, the big man leaned over and addressed the young people across from him. "You work here, don't you?" he asked loudly.

"Yes, we do," Kelvin answered, pointing to the opposite side of the building. "We sell meat for Lanning's Foods over there, every Tuesday and Friday."

The big man glanced around and then turned back again. "So that's where I saw you before," he said. "I knew I'd seen this young lady somewhere." He nodded toward Rosalie. "I want to say something to you."

Rosalie blushed, and Kelvin looked at her over the top of the lunch box between them. Kelvin unscrewed the lid of his thermos, and Rosalie nearly choked on her sandwich. Then, before either of them could speak, the big man went on.

"My name is Douglas Ambrose, and I'm a born-again believer—praise the Lord," he announced. "So that makes us the same, doesn't it?"

Kelvin took a spoonful of bean soup and swallowed it. "Well, that depends," he began carefully.

"Depends on what?" the big man wanted to know. "I've been filled with the Spirit, and I and my wife"—he stopped and corrected himself—"I and my current companion are finding joy in the Lord. Isn't that enough?"

Kelvin took another spoonful of soup and frowned, trying to think of an answer. He glanced at Rosalie, but she bowed her head. Douglas followed his glance and cleared his throat.

"Day after tomorrow," he said, "I'm leaving on a business trip to Bolivia. I'll be gone, oh, maybe a year or two and make lots of money. And when I return, I'm going to become a Mennonite like you. I want to belong to a church where the women look like you," he said, indicating Rosalie, "and where the men are brave and strong like you," he added, nodding at Kelvin.

Kelvin looked surprised. "In what way do you mean?"

Douglas settled back in his seat and nodded at Rosalie again. "I believe that's the Biblical way to dress. Besides, it makes a woman look more beautiful." Rosalie kept her face averted from his direct gaze, and he nodded in approval. "And I like a shy one. It's more right, somehow."

Then he turned his attention back to Kelvin. "Now, let's say I want to become a part of your church. Where would I need to reform?" He waited expectantly.

"Well, for one thing, you would need a genuine new birth experience," Kelvin answered.

"Which I already have," Douglas stated confidently. "What's next?"

Kelvin paused. This stranger seemed so sure of himself. Then he said, "After you've attended for long enough to make sure this is what you want—"

"It *is* what I want," Douglas cut in.

"And after we've had a time of proving, to see whether you show the fruits of a godly life—"

"But that's judging," Douglas interrupted. "The Bible tells us not to judge."

"Yes," Kelvin agreed. "But Jesus Himself said that a man is known by his fruits. We want to keep our church pure. So we'd need to see what kind of fruit your life produces."

A worried look crossed the man's face, but he nodded again. "I can understand that. What's next?"

"And then you would likely go through a time of instruction—"

"You mean—like—like brainwashing?" Douglas sputtered. "You mean everyone in your church has to believe exactly like you do before they become members?" He sounded astonished.

"Well, yes, pretty well," Kelvin answered. "We want to believe only what the Bible teaches, of course. If you also believe what the Bible teaches, then we can probably agree."

"But that's—that's not fair!" Douglas burst out. "What if I do believe the Bible, but still disagree with you? Would that keep me from joining your church?"

Kelvin turned the thermos on end to pour out the last of the beans. "Grant me wisdom, dear Lord," he prayed.

Then he looked up to meet Douglas's troubled gaze. "What did you have in mind?" he asked.

"Well," Douglas replied, squirming, "I understand you don't accept divorced and remarried people."

Kelvin shook his head. "We have accepted some like that," he replied. "But they needed to renounce their sins and live separately, since we believe such marriages are wrong, according to the Bible."

"But that's not fair," Douglas repeated. "And

would you really tear apart a happy marriage just for your beliefs?"

He turned to Rosalie. "What would you do if they'd tear you away from your husband?"

Rosalie looked at Kelvin. "But the Bible says that those relationships are wrong," Kelvin answered.

"Oh, I know what the Bible says, and I'm sorry for the sins I've done in the past," Douglas said. "But now my current relationship is happy. In fact, she wants to get married and become a Mennonite with me." A note of challenge crept into his voice. "You wouldn't turn away potential members, would you?"

"But the Bible still says—"

Douglas waved his hand in Kelvin's face. Then he rose to his feet and looked down on the two young people. "I admire your answers," he said. "You seem to know what your church believes. But I'm afraid I wouldn't fit in. Thanks for your time anyway."

Watching him go, Kelvin shook his head sadly. "I'm afraid," he said to Rosalie, "that Douglas would like to be a Mennonite without becoming a Bible-believing Christian. And there is too much of a difference."

31

Truck for Sale

Come right on in, neighbor. Good thing you caught me in the house. Most days I'd be out in my fields by now, but this rain keeps me stuck in here. Sure, come on out to the kitchen and visit awhile. Can I pour you some coffee? My wife sure does make good coffee, doesn't she.

Actually, I haven't seen you very often yet. What is it, three weeks since you moved in across the road? Something like that anyway. You're living in the same house David Lehman used to live in before he moved out to Manitoba. You don't know David Lehman, do you? Well, you don't know what you're missing, I guess. But you sure missed one of the beautiful people God created, when you missed him. He was the kindest and most honest man I ever met.

What was that? You ask me how do I know he was honest? Well, how do you know I'm sitting here beside you? You can see me, right? And hear me? I don't need to tell you every minute that I am here. You'd get mad at me for that, eh? Well, David simply *was* kind and honest. He just naturally did the things people liked. Any way you looked at him, you couldn't find an unkind streak in him. And I mean that. . . .

You want to know where he went to church? He went to that little, white Mennonite church over on the other side of Springfield. As regular as a clock, every Sunday morning he'd go. Sunday evenings and Wednesday evenings besides. And even sometimes for a whole week in a row. I never knew how a person could stand so much church, but it sure didn't hurt him.

Or his wife either, for that matter. She could bake the best pies I ever did eat, and she wasn't stingy about sharing them. Me and the missis, we used to just sorta drop in every once in a while when we knew it was mealtime at the Lehmans'. Oh, the things that lady could do with some flour and a few cherries! They'd make you feel delicious right to the roots of your toes.

But let me get back to David. There comes a

day one time when he's hard up for some cash. Of course, that's no surprise; it happens to the best of us. But do you think he would borrow anything? Not him. He told me once he didn't like debts, and he wouldn't make more of 'em than he could possibly help. So what do you think he does when he needs more money? He puts his truck up for sale! His truck that he uses almost every day, mind you. . . .

Why does he need the money? Oh, maybe I forgot to tell you. His little boy got his foot caught under a cow when she decided to sit down. Broke it up bad. Three pins they had to put in, and he stayed for over a month in the hospital over in Shiloh. And David, good man that he is, doesn't even have health insurance, so of course he pays the whole works out of his own pocket. I couldn't do it myself, but I must admit I admire him for it.

Well, anyway, the bills about eat him up, and he needs more money quick to make mortgage payments. So he puts his truck up for sale. Real nice pickup it is too. He always keeps his vehicles in good shape, being handy with a wrench and all that. So this truck should have been worth about five thousand, easy. But he says he doesn't want to give anybody a bad deal, so he only asks four thousand for it. I'd have bought it myself if I could have, but I didn't need it anyhow, and I didn't have that much extra money either. So it sits there by the road for about a week, and nobody even looks at it.

Finally I walk across the road one day. "David," I says, "you're not asking enough for that truck out there. People are scared there's something wrong with it, such a good-looking thing and all. If you'd ask more for it, you'd likely sell it faster."

He is hoeing corn that day, and I still remember how he leans on his hoe and smiles one of his widest smiles, the kind that makes me wish I could be so calm and peaceful in everything like he is. Well, after he smiles for a bit, he gives me this real nice talk about how his God is so kind to him and how he's sure if the truck is supposed to sell, it will sell. And in the meantime he's going to keep busy praying and working. Never saw the likes of that fellow, that I didn't. His religion must be really something if he can keep himself calm like that and not even worry about anything when he knows he's just about as strapped as he can be.

Anyway, on the very next day, here comes this man, chugging along in a real nice car, tinted windows and everything. Looks about as rich as can be, and he's interested in this truck.

Now, I'm sorta interested to see how this turns out, so it happens I've got to trim my rosebushes in the corner of the yard by the road right then.

From there, I can hear real good.

This rich-looking man wants the truck, and he can talk real smooth, as smooth as oil when it's spilled on the floor. He explains all about how he was just driving in the area—doesn't usually come through here, but today he's got business here— and he's seen this truck, and he'd like to buy it and take it back with him. Sounds believable, and he looks like the kind of man who'd do things right now if he felt like it. Happens he's even got his wife with him, so he can drive the truck away on the spot. . . .

How's that? You mean how'd he come past here in the first place? Well, I can see what you're getting at. This here isn't any main road, that's for sure. Looking back now, I wonder if he didn't see the truck here one other day and came back later for it, seeing as he wanted it real bad. . . .

Now, just hang on a bit, and we'll get to it all by and by. This man in the ritzy car, he whips out a checkbook and writes a check, right then and there. And he writes it for the whole sum, four thousand, flat out. Doesn't even argue, just says he figures it's a good price for a good truck.

So anyway, before long he leans down in his car and tells his wife she's got to drive the car now because he's going to drive this truck home. Now, just between me and you, let me tell you this. Most times David is about as alert as can be and real sharp at catching on to things. I'm surprised he didn't suspect right then that this fellow was up to some trick, what with his smooth talk and his big money and his grand hurry.

So anyway, the lady drives the fancy car, and the man gets in the truck and starts it and drives off.

David stands there and watches him go, and then he sees me fiddling around by the fence, and he comes across the road. "I sold my truck," he says to me, pleased as can be.

"I seen that," I tell him. "Are you going to take that check to the bank right away? I sure would if I was you."

He holds up the check and squints at it, and then he puts it in his shirt pocket. "No," he says, "I've got to finish hoeing my corn, or all at once it'll be drowned in the weeds. This can wait until tomorrow."

So he wants to wait another day to get hold of all that money. Well, I've got to be nice to the fellow, so I agree with him, and we both go back to our work.

Next day, I see David and his wife and the children leave for town, all of 'em smiling as wide as they can. I'm working out in the garden beside the road, and when he stops by the fence, I go and see what he wants.

He shows me the check and asks if I know where to find that bank in town. Bank of Nova Scotia it was, and I tell him how to find it. I remember the name on the check too: Orville Gilbert. Such a high-sounding name, and I didn't even recognize it, except for the man I'd seen the day before. . . .

Why would I recognize it, you ask? Well, I just kind of get around and find things out. If there'd be somebody so rich as that anywhere around, I'd likely find out sooner or later. So I decide this Orville Gilbert must not be from around here.

Well, I go back to my garden, and David goes to town to cash his check that's going to get him out of trouble. But it doesn't take long, and he comes back again, and he's not smiling anymore. He goes in the house, and pretty soon he comes out with a hoe, and he starts hoeing corn again just as fast as he knows how. And I can't figure it out. So after a bit, my shovel handle kind of breaks, and I trot on over to see if I could borrow his for a day or so.

"So, David," I says when I find him in the field, "I see you're back already."

He looks up from his corn, and I see he's been crying. Well, that makes me embarrassed, and I don't know what to say right off. But he looks me straight in the eye and says, "Yes, I'm back. But

I'm afraid I can't stay here very long anymore."

Now I'm more astonished than ever, and the only thing I can think of to say is "Whatever?"

"Yes, I'm afraid it's so," he says. "That check is no good, and now my truck is gone. It's still almost three months until harvest, and the mortgage is two months behind already. We've got to live on something. I've already talked to my father, and he offered his tenant house for us to live in until we find another place we can afford." . . .

You ask what happened to the check? I'm wondering the same thing, of course. Turns out there's nobody like Orville Gilbert, at least not in the bank's records. David even went all the way to the address at the top of the check, and there's not even such an address. Talk about a rubber check! This one wasn't just rubber, it was more like foam.

Of course, I am angry right away and tell David all kinds of ways to make sure he gets the fellow back.

But he just smiles and shakes his head. First off, he don't believe in suing, so that's out. He's already told the police about it, but they don't have much hope of finding the truck. Could easy be painted by now, for one thing, and they'd have to look anywhere from here to California, seeing as the man deliberately did something crooked to get hold of it. Then David asks me, "So how do you track a person down when he likely isn't even using his own name? How do you know he won't be using a different name by the time you find him?"

Well, he's got a point there, so I leave him be, even if I think he's crazy to do it like that. Not so many days after that, I notice they're packing up. Then one day a truck comes and takes them all away, and David Lehman lives here no more.

And then, of course, sooner or later you come along and buy the place from the fellow who repossessed it. And here we are, good neighbors already.

But do you know what? The more I think about it, the more I admire David Lehman. It takes a tremendous amount more strength to take a loss and be quiet about it than it does to walk off with a pickup that's not even yours. Yes sir, David Lehman did the right thing, even if I couldn't have done it like he did. . . .

No, you can't mean that. I could have the same strength David did? Impossible. You can't make a saint out of a fellow like me. Saints like David are born, not made. . . .

Are you sure? By the blood of Jesus Christ, you say? Well, David talked to me about it a couple of times, but I didn't really listen—figured he didn't know what he was talking about, seeing as he'd been born a saint. . . .

You say he wasn't? How do you know? You

never knew David, did you? . . .

You weren't born a saint either? Hmm. I haven't seen much of you, but I must admit you're a lot like David. But no way could I be like him. I don't know how. . . .

How's that? You're going to the same church David went to? Really now? And you want me to come too? I'll think about that. Any church that has people like David Lehman can't be all bad. Tell you what, I think maybe I'll wait a few weeks and see if it's really true you're going to be the same kind as David. If you are, I'll come and see what it's all about. If you're not, well, I'm going to be disappointed. You see what I mean?

32

Which God?

In the early days of the missions in northern Ontario, the church sent a certain young missionary and his wife to embark upon the unknown adventures of the bush country. The love of God in their hearts prompted them to live as close to their Indian friends as they could. For a winter and a summer, they had lived among the natives of the northland, but the people about them seemed very aloof. It did not matter that the white man's cottage was no larger than theirs or that the white man had learned to eat the foods they loved. The Indians still insisted that their Manitou was just as great as the white man's strange God. In their minds, there was no need to provoke their Manitou to anger by leaving the ways of their forefathers for this new, untried way of the white man.

Toward dawn on a winter morning, near the end of the second winter that the white man had witnessed in these parts, a fine mist rose from the shores of Pickle Lake. The bare birch and poplar trees crackled and groaned in the bitter cold. Some minutes later, the rays of the sun spread over the edge of the frozen landscape and illuminated a ring of huts among the trees on the shoreline. Some of the huts sprouted thin, straight lines of blue smoke into the weak sunshine. Those were the homes where hunger and cold had overcome the clutches of blankets and sleep. Soon, now, the village would waken to life, though there was not much activity at this time of year. All communication with the outside world must be over the lake, which was a precarious business at best in the days when snow and ice held the world in subjection.

In a small house near the end of the row, a young man stood gazing out the hole that he had blown in the frost on the windowpane. He had only intended to check the temperature, but now the sun shone brightly on his fair hair, and still he stood there. His thoughts were far away, but he came back with a start when his wife tapped him on the shoulder. "Breakfast is ready, Jonathan," she told him softly. "Let's eat before the porridge gets cold."

"Yes, Bessie," he replied. "Let me get my Bible. We have time for our devotions first."

"Of course," Bessie agreed. She seated herself beside the small table that held not much more than a large pot of steaming porridge. She had long ago decided that if her neighbors could be content with little, so could she. The joy in her heart was evident on her beaming face as she waited for Jonathan to find the passage for their morning reading.

Jonathan's voice rose and fell as he read again the beloved Shepherd Psalm. When he finished, he paused for just a bit and then bowed his head in prayer. Was there an extra fervor in his voice this morning? Bessie could not be quite sure. "And, Lord, whatever it takes," Jonathan was saying, "help me to get close to these dear people and to show them that You are indeed a greater God than Manitou. Help me somehow to reach inside their hearts with Your love and to bring them to an understanding of You."

When the prayer had ended, Jonathan scooped his bowl full of delicious cooked grain. "The thermometer shows thirty below this morning," he announced to Bessie. "That will freeze the ice road

over the lake again after those three days of thawing weather we had."

Bessie nodded. "Spring will be here soon, hope-
fully," she stated. "It seems strange to say that at
the beginning of March. At home, my mother likely
has her garden nearly planted already."

Jonathan chuckled deep in his throat. "Not
much use planting a garden here right now," he
commented. "Unless indeed you would like to lose
the seed down in the snowbanks." He helped himself to a piece of cold bannock. "I think today might
be a good day to fetch the little tractor that we left
on Two Beaver Island. Remember, we took the
Belarus over there to use in making firewood during the winter?"

"How could I forget that!" Bessie said, laughing. "I thought for sure you would fall through
the ice and never come back up again. But that
was before I learned how thick and strong these
ice roads become."

"Thick and strong is right," Jonathan agreed.
"I never would have believed it if I hadn't seen
with my own eyes that the ice reaches three feet
thick where it isn't protected by snow. By that
time, going across the lake is no problem, as long
as you stay on the road and don't freeze yourself."

Bessie shivered. "Let's not talk about freezing,"
she said. "I don't need a very strong imagination

for that right now." She rose and put another piece of wood into the fire. Then they ate the rest of their breakfast in silence while Jonathan planned the day's trip to the island in the middle of their lake.

"I guess I'll take Albert along," Jonathan stated finally. "He never has much to say, but he's good with engines. If I'd need any help getting the tractor started, he might be useful. Besides, someone will need to bring the snowmobile back if I drive the tractor."

"Will you need any lunch?" Bessie asked. "I could wrap up a few moose-meat sandwiches if you'd like."

Jonathan shook his head and started toward the closet. "It shouldn't take more than a few hours," he said. "But I'll likely be glad for a hot dinner by and by. Could you bring me those two pairs of woolen socks from the bottom dresser drawer?"

"Surely," Bessie answered. A minute later, she stood beside him as he pulled on layer after layer of clothes. Her eyes grew larger as she watched. "Whatever are you thinking?" she asked. "Three pairs of socks and three pairs of pants, plus those fur outer pants. And a sweater and a woolen shirt and a flannel shirt besides the two you usually wear. How will you ever get into your fur parka?"

"Oh, I'll stuff myself in," Jonathan answered lightly. Then he turned to face her. "Somehow I feel an urgency to put lots of clothes on today," he said seriously. "All kinds of things can happen so far across the lake on a cold day like this. Not that we'll necessarily break through, of course, because the ice is strong. But let's pray again before I start out."

Together the two knelt while Jonathan once more prayed earnestly for grace to witness to those he would meet that day. "Show Yourself to them through us somehow, Lord. And keep us safe in Your care today. In Jesus' Name. Amen."

Jonathan found Albert at the first place he looked, lounging beside the stove in the trading post at the opposite end of the village. When he explained the errand of the day, Albert opened his eyes a bit wider, but he did not say anything. Jonathan was not surprised; Albert was one of the quietest people he had ever met.

While he waited for Albert to go and fetch another parka, Jonathan chatted with the circle of Indians around the stove. When Albert returned, the two men declined the offer of hot coffee and set out to a chorus of "See you later" and "Come back soon" from the open door of the trading post. Jonathan smiled to himself. For all their reluctance about accepting the white man's God, these people had no problem being friendly to the white man himself.

The two men on the snowmobile produced an amazing picture. Knowing the ways of winter travel, Jonathan had brought along half a dozen blankets in order to have enough for both him and Albert. Some of them he would need for the return trip. However, they still needed to take all of them along now. By the time all the blankets had been wrapped around both men, they looked like a giant papoose skating over the lake on a remarkably agile sled.

The half-hour trip across the lake proved uneventful. Several times, the aging snowmobile sputtered and threatened to stall, but it kept on going. And when Jonathan and his passenger reached Two Beaver Island, the little Belarus still sat just where they had left it the last time they had cut wood. By now it was cold and stiff, so they worked over it for nearly an hour before it started. With the tractor put-putting reassuringly, the two men prepared to return across the ice road.

While they waited a few minutes for the engine to warm, Jonathan suddenly decided to transfer the tools from the toolbox on the tractor into the compartment at the end of the snowmobile. Albert watched, silent as always. With that operation completed, Jonathan wrapped himself in half of the blankets, climbed onto the tractor, and eased it down the ramp onto the ice. The sun shone brilliantly on the dazzling white snow, making Jonathan squint in order to see the path between the snowbanks.

Albert watched him go, and then he turned to the snowmobile and tried to start it. It sputtered and hiccupped, but it did not start. The Indian's dark face puckered in thought. Another try produced the same results. Pondering his situation, Albert sat down on the seat of the machine and followed Jonathan's progress with his eyes. What he saw made him gasp in horror.

Jonathan had traveled several hundred feet by now. Just before he rounded a bend in the road, he turned back to check if Albert was following him. Seeing that Albert sat on the snowmobile without moving it, Jonathan stared for a bit longer, trying to figure out just what the problem might be. The steady travel of the tractor brought him closer and closer to the ridge of snow that marked the edge of the ice road. Suddenly the tractor crawled over the ridge and started across the uncharted whiteness beyond.

Feeling something different, Jonathan swung his head around just in time to see what was happening. But he cranked the steering wheel around too late. The front right wheel traveled across an air pocket. With a sickening crack, that wheel disappeared into the ice. Then, before Jonathan could react, the hole in the ice enlarged, and the rest of the tractor broke through into the cold, black water underneath.

Thinking quickly, Jonathan took a large gulp of air just before the water closed over the top of him. Down, down, down he went, into the darkness below. Things seemed to happen in slow motion. As the rocks on the bottom rose to meet him, Jonathan struggled with the blankets that were still wrapped about his legs. "Oh, God, help me now," he prayed quickly. Before his eyes, he could see Bessie's face, and a stab went through his heart. "Bring me out of here if it is Your will," he prayed again. "Bessie needs me, and the Indians haven't seen the light yet. Please, God."

By that time he had reached the end of the descent. As he felt the slight jolt of the tractor hitting bottom, the last fold of blanket fell away from him. Looking upward, he saw a vast darkness with a popcorn seed of light almost directly overhead. Then he felt himself being forced upward. Below him, the tractor with its odd canopy of blankets became smaller and smaller. Above him, the point of light became larger until he could see the ragged edges where the tractor had broken through. He reached for it, trying to aim his body toward that hole and deliverance.

After what seemed like hours, Jonathan felt

himself suddenly thrust out of the hole and bounced aside. "Praise the Lord!" he shouted, almost before his eyes could focus again. "Thank You, God!" He staggered a bit and then stood up straight on the ice road.

A startled grunt in front of him made Jonathan wipe the water from his face and look. There stood Albert, wide-eyed and speechless with astonishment. After he had seen Jonathan disappear, he had frantically worked over his machine until it finally started. Then, in tears, he had roared over the intervening ice.

In that short space of time, Albert had suddenly realized just how precious this white man and his message had become. In the last several months, Albert had spent much time pondering what the white man had to say. Now, to his great alarm, he knew that he was the only person in the whole vast wilderness who had witnessed the end of the white man. What would he say to his people? How could he explain what had happened? And what would they do without this kind, thoughtful neighbor? Albert had just alighted from his snowmobile and walked over to the hole when that same white man, somehow, came bounding out of the hole again, very much alive and shouting to his God.

Before Albert could react to such an astounding turn of events, Jonathan ran to the snowmobile.

"Take me back to the trading post," he shouted. "I'm all wet; can't you see?" Already his clothes were crackling with cold.

The sound of Jonathan's shout seemed to wake up Albert. He took his place in front of Jonathan and pulled the remaining blankets around them both. And then, as if afraid of that place, he roared as fast as he could down the glittering road toward the village and the trading post. From this direction, the trading post would be the first building they would reach.

In no time at all, Jonathan's clothes froze solid. However, he suddenly realized the value of the layers and layers that he had put on that morning. The layer next to his skin was damp, but not wet. As soon as the outer layers froze, they made a shell nearly as hard as iron, which effectively kept the cold air from entering and chilling his body. Several times, Albert turned and shouted above the sound of the engine, "Cold yet?"

"No," Jonathan would reply and then chuckle at the disbelief in Albert's face. Albert clearly did not believe that a person just out of the lake on a day like this could possibly stay warm. *Just wait,* Jonathan thought, *just wait until I have a chance to tell him how my God brought me out of that water and how He kept me from freezing even when I hadn't expected to break through.*

By the time they arrived at the trading post, Jonathan was just starting to shiver. Albert hailed the assorted collection of shoppers and coffee drinkers who had gathered. In an unusual burst of language, he started giving orders. "You there," he said, pointing, "you go and stuff that old stove full of birch logs and heat a tub of water. And you and you and you, come help me carry this fellow inside. He almost drowned. And you"—he pointed to his son—"go fetch my sharp knife to cut off his clothes. We'll have to get this man into a tub of hot water as fast as we can."

"No, no, no," Jonathan protested. "I'm fine. Don't cut my clothes off. I'll be all right. Just let me thaw out, and I'll be fine. Please. I'm sure. Just leave my clothes alone."

In spite of his arguments, four men picked him up bodily, since his frozen clothes prevented him from walking, and deposited him on the floor beside the stove. By his much talking, Jonathan finally persuaded them not to take a knife to his clothes.

As welcome warmth began soaking in and thawing the ice shell around him, they helped him to peel the layers off, one by one. The circle of faces around him stared in wonder as layers kept appearing. Finally, Chief Crow Talk asked the questions that bothered them all. "Who told you how many clothes to put on this morning? Do you know that those layers and layers saved your life? If you hadn't been protected like a ptarmigan with its feathers, you would have frozen long before you came back here."

That was what Jonathan had waited for. He launched into a detailed account of the workings of his God, especially of how God leads His children in paths they do not know. As he described his experience under the ice, the wonder on the dark faces around him slowly changed to amazement.

What kind of God was so interested in His children that He would move a man to put on so many clothes, even if that man would not normally have done so? Did He really care enough about details that He would give a man the impulse to move all his tools to safety? All of them knew the importance and scarcity of a good set of tools in this country. And how could this God guide a gush of water to save a man's life? Moreover, this God had evidently overcome the laws of nature that they were all acquainted with—had He not brought Jonathan out of the water when he was weighted down with waterlogged clothes? Was this the kind of love that Jonathan had been speaking about all these months?

By the time the last damp layer had been peeled off, Jonathan was glad for the warm blanket that appeared as if out of nowhere. And while he waited for enough clothes to dry so that he could go home, he kept on talking. Never before had his audience been so receptive to his message. He felt sure that Bessie would not mind a late dinner for such a reason.

As time went on, other brethren and sisters came to assist in the work. The brethren sensed a new respect toward them and the message of the Gospel. First Albert, then one by one several more Indians came, asking the brethren to teach them how they should behave for this God. Before very long, it was Jonathan's great joy to instruct a class of not one or two but six men in preparation for baptism. Their testimonies were thrilling, but Jonathan was often sobered as he thought about the incident that had opened their eyes. For the time being, the tractor would stay on the bottom of the lake. And as Jonathan reflected on it, he no longer cared whether he ever saw it again. What was one little tractor worth, compared to the souls of these Indian friends? If this was the way God had chosen to bring His love into their hearts, what could Jonathan say against it?